AMERICAN CATHOLIC PREACHING AND PIETY IN THE TIME OF JOHN CARROLL

MELVILLE STUDIES IN CHURCH HISTORY

FROM

The Department of Church History
The Catholic University of America

EDITED BY

Nelson H. Minnich

EDITORIAL COMMITTEE

John Tracy Ellis   Jacques M. Gres-Gayer
Robert B. Eno, S.S.   Robert Trisco

MELVILLE STUDIES IN CHURCH HISTORY
VOLUME II

AMERICAN CATHOLIC PREACHING AND PIETY IN THE TIME OF JOHN CARROLL

Raymond J. Kupke
Editor

UNIVERSITY
PRESS OF
AMERICA

Lanham • New York • London

The Department of
Church History

The Catholic University
of America

BX
4705
.C33
A54
1990

Copyright © 1991 by

University Press of America®, Inc.

4720 Boston Way
Lanham, Maryland 20706

3 Henrietta Street
London WC2E 8LU England

Co-published by arrangement with The Department of Church History,
The Catholic University of America

Library of Congress Cataloging-in-Publication Data

American Catholic preaching and piety
in the time of John Carroll.
p.   cm. — (Melville studies in church history ; v. 2)
Includes bibliographical references and index.
1. Carroll, John, 1735-1815.   2. Preaching—
United States—History.   3. Spirituality—Catholic
Church—History.   I. Kupke, Raymond J.   II. Series.
BX4705.C33A54   1990
252'.0273'09033—dc20   90–22864 CIP

ISBN 0–8191–8121–8 (hard : alk. paper)

The paper used in this publication meets the minimum requirements of
American National Standard for Information Sciences—Permanence
of Paper for Printed Library Materials, ANSI Z39.48–1984.

To Nelson H. Minnich
teacher, mentor, friend

"A teacher affects eternity;
he can never tell where his influence stops."
The Education of Henry Adams

Acknowledgment

Monsignor John Tracy Ellis' autobiography was the first in a projected series of studies in church history. This volume is the second. The series bears the name of Dr. Annabelle M. Melville, an alumna of the Catholic University of America, distinguished historian of the Catholic Church in America, and Commonwealth Professor Emerita of History, Bridgewater State College, Massachusetts, since 1977. Her generous benefactions to the Department of Church History make possible the publication of a series of monographs featuring the work of the faculty, students, and alumni/ae of this department. It is hoped that these studies will carry on the tradition of exacting scholarship and deep love for the history of the Church so well exemplified in the career and writings of Dr. Melville.

Table of Contents

INTRODUCTION   xi
Charles Edwards O'Neill, S.J.

JOHN CARROLL, THE "CATHOLIC
ENLIGHTENMENT" AND ROME   1
Charles Edwards O'Neill, S.J.

THE EUCHARIST AS PRESENTED IN THE
CORPUS CHRISTI SERMONS OF COLONIAL
ANGLO-AMERICA   27
Joseph C. Linck

DEAREST CHRISTIANS: A STUDY OF
EIGHTEENTH CENTURY ANGLO-AMERICAN
CATHOLIC ECCLESIOLOGY   55
Raymond J. Kupke

MARIAN SPIRITUALITY IN EARLY AMERICA   87
Michael Sean Winters

JOHN CARROLL AND THE ENLIGHTENMENT   107
Carla Bang

APPENDIX   137
Selections from the American Catholic Sermon
Collection

INDEX   213

John Carroll (1735–1815), first bishop (1789–1808) and archbishop (1808– 1815) of Baltimore. Founder of the Catholic hierarchy in the United States of America. (Gilbert Stuart portrait courtesy of Georgetown University).

Introduction

Charles Edwards O'Neill, S.J.

Two hundred years ago John Carroll was ordained bishop. The Maryland-born Irish-American had gone to Europe as a boy (1748) for his education, had entered the Society of Jesus (1753), and been ordained a priest (1769). After the suppression of the Jesuit order (1773) Carroll returned to his family home (1774), somewhat disillusioned, but still dedicated to the sacred ministry. In the 1780s he emerged as a leader among his brethren, both by their and Rome's choice.

In this bicentennial year of his episcopal ordination there are several reasons for publishing a study of the piety and preaching of John Carroll's day. First, historical writing, after long study of ecclesiastical structures and numbers, has in recent years turned to examine spirituality and personal religious living in so far as it can be known. Second, although some work has been published on nineteenth-century Catholic piety in the United States, no volume, to my knowledge, has appeared on eighteenth-century American Catholic piety. Thirdly, a bit of cloud has arisen over a few terms and themes; so it is worthwhile to help clarify them.

During the spring of 1989 a seminar group at The Catholic University of America met to study America Catholic piety and preaching in the colonial and early national periods.

Sources are less abundant for the pre-1800 years than, say, for the nineteenth century. Nonetheless, three of the seminar participants found ample material in the manuscript sermons found in three collections at the Georgetown University Library; a fourth student examined the published sermons of John Carroll. In the seminar we found that some currently accepted expressions and views in American Catholic historiography would benefit from revision.

For example, some devotional attitudes that have been presented as a development that followed the nineteenth-century waves of immigration can be found present in the eighteenth century. One would, of course, expect a degree of devotional development to take place when millions of people are involved over several decades. Nonetheless, what the young scholars found is noteworthy in regard to ecclesiology, Eucharistic piety and Marian devotion. They concluded that some who have written about the contrast between later and earlier Catholic piety would wish to revise their views if they knew the earlier period better. Their papers:

Joseph Linck examined Eucharistic doctrine and devotion in the colonial sermons.

Raymond Kupke analyzed the ecclesiology of the preachers.

Sean Michael Winters followed their Marian doctrine and devotion.

The fourth participant Carla Bang, analyzing the corpus of sermons left by John Carroll, showed how strongly he denounced the ideas which are usually associated with the Enlightenment.

The first three of these papers formed a session of the spring meeting of the American Catholic Historical Association on April 7, 1990, at Loyola College in Baltimore. Loyola Professor Thomas M. McCoog chaired the session, and Georgetown Professor R. Emmett Curran commented—favorably, I am told—on the new perspectives offered by the trio.

As presenter of their papers for this bicentennial publication, I contribute in these pages an analysis of John Carroll and Rome, and of John Carroll and the 'Catholic Enlightenment.' The question the essay faces is whether and to what extent in his personal thought and teaching John Carroll drew upon the currents of the "Catholic Enlightenment."

When Patricia Bonomi studied the formation of American religious culture, she found that her sources required a change in the way many summarized eighteenth-century North American Protestant thought. As she concluded, "an eighteenth century of 'Enlightenment' skepticism coming between a 'Puritan' seventeenth century and an 'evangelical' nineteenth century simply does not add up."[1] At the conclusion of the above-mentioned seminar the participants asked themselves whether, *mutatis mutandis,* some similar restructuring may not be called for in the study of eighteenth- and nineteenth-century Catholic preaching and piety. With this volume they invite readers to join in the questioning.

---

1. Patricia U. Bonomi, *Under the Cape of Heaven. Religion, Society and Politics in Colonial America* (New York, 1986), p. 220.

John Carroll, the "Catholic Enlightenment" and Rome

Charles Edwards O'Neill

Within the present volume Carla Bang shows how strongly John Carroll preached against the philosophical, religious ideas commonly grouped under the heading of "the Enlightenment." Although the average author, reader or speaker takes the term as embracing the ideas examined in her paper, one can find an extended use of the term in the expression "Catholic Enlightenment." This altered use of the term excludes, of course, the anti-theistic, anti-Christian, anti-Church views of a Denis Diderot or a Voltaire.

Joseph P. Chinnici has written of the "English Catholic Enlightenment."[1]

The *Lexicon für Theologie und Kirche* finds interrelated Enlightenment facets and Catholic currents.[2]

The Italian peninsula had *prelati illuminati* in the time of Scipione de' Ricci (1741–1810), bishop of Pistoia and Prato.[3]

In twentieth-century France *"Aufklärung catholique"* is the two-language term used by Bernard Plongeron in his study of "political theology" at the end of the eighteenth century and beginning of the nineteenth. But the "Catholic Enlightenment," he found, was made up of different currents and did not have a central synthesis.[4] Significantly, though, the expression "Catholic Enlightenment" does not appear in the recent (September 1989) essay of Daniel Roche on themes and currents at the end of the *ancien régime*.[5]

Spanish historians are currently discussing the issue of the "Enlightenment" in Spain. In the latest Espasa-Calpe survey of Spanish history, Teófanes Egido, challenging earlier presentations, maintains that the Enlightenment figures in Spain were far from irreligious.[6] Yet more recently, Rafael Olaechea questions whether the term *ilustrado* can be applied in any usual sense of the word to the Spanish "reformers" of the reign of Carlos III; the Zaragoza professor judges that Spain's developers and development were so different that the use of the expression *Enlightenment,* borrowed from elsewhere, is misleading.[7]

With the term "Catholic Enlightenment" one enters a world of mobile definitions. Assuredly every one can give a term a new meaning. In England the word *cisalpine,* drawn from an ancient Latin adjective, meant "related to the area south of the Alps." Since, though, a group of Catholics in the early nineteenth century wished to assert an anti-ultramontane position, they turned *cisalpine* around to mean the very opposite of what it had meant in English since at least mid-sixteenth century.[8]

In the limited scope of these pages one cannot take in the whole sweep of terms and themes involved. So let us stay close to John Carroll, who in the past decade has come to be seen as "an Enlightenment bishop." James Hennesey in 1978 stated that John Carroll's "Europe was that of the Enlightenment" and that "John Carroll was a man of his time."[9] Hennesey stopped short, however, of fusing the predicates. In more recent publications it has become commonplace to link John Carroll's name with the Enlightenment. For example:

Jay P. Dolan, in *The American Catholic Experience* (New

York, 1985), p. 102, asserts that "John Carroll certainly shared this Enlightenment mentality" received through "English Catholic thinkers."

Patrick Carey, with nuanced distinctions, connects John Carroll and American "Enlightenment Catholicism" in *American Catholic Religious Thought: The Shaping of a Theological and Social Tradition* (New York, 1987), pp. 5–15.

Robert Emmett Curran, has a chapter entitled "John Carroll and Enlightened Catholicism" in his anthology *American Jesuit Spirituality. The Maryland Tradition, 1634–1900* (New York, 1988).

David O'Brien, "Dissent in American Catholicism," *Records of the American Catholic Historical Society of Philadelphia,* 99 (1988) 56, speaks of John Carroll's "enlightenment piety."

Joseph P. Chinnici in *Living Stones. The History and Structure of Catholic Spiritual Life in the United States* (New York, 1989) calls Part One, which ends with Carroll's death, "An Enlightenment Synthesis, 1776–1815."

Let us avoid a *lis de verbis* and accept the terms and definitions the several authors prefer. Next let us take the ensemble of concepts which are usually associated with what is called "Catholic Enlightenment"—as distinct from the more common meaning of the Enlightenment. Then let us see John Carroll's appreciation of those concepts and his reaction to them. Having surveyed the field, I choose the following themes as being characteristic of the "Catholic Enlightenment." Someone else might add or subtract one or two concepts. I recognize the problem, for, like *renaissance,* the *enlightenment* is stretched or restricted by different authors. I invite the reader to follow through this construct, because, it seems to me, the conclusion does not depend upon one or two of the ideas, but rather upon the ensemble. Let us look for John Carroll's view regarding:

1. A sense of modern times and current ideas, that is to say "Enlightenment"; praise of Reason and rational thinking;
2. Liberty and revolution;
3. "Enlightened despotism," with an ecclesiastical policy associated with Joseph II or Febronius.
4. Gallicanism; or similar "episcopalism";
5. Apology for Jansenism, with a positive attitude toward the Synod of Pistoia and a negative attitude toward the Society of Jesus and devotion to the Sacred Heart of Jesus;
6. Religious tolerance.
7. Expressions—beyond 4 and 5—of anti-Roman feeling.

1. John Carroll almost never uses the word *enlightened*. When he does, he gives it the common rather than the special meaning. He refers to St. John Chrysostom as "that enlightened doctor."[10] And Carroll writes of the "enlightened zeal" of his friend Charles Plowden.[11]

Carroll favored serious study of language and science, but his statements in this area are independent of any particular age.[12] Carroll's promotion of education is rooted rather in his Jesuit background than in any particular contemporary movement. In Carroll's view school work was what Jesuits had done best; he favored education for traditional reasons. He criticized the kind of speech-making "which border[ed] too much on the affected philosophical language of infidelity, by paying too many compliments to the superior wisdom and light of the present times."[13]

Carroll worried about what his priest-friend Joseph Berington might write in a work—in the event, never published—on the papacy, because Carroll feared that Berington would "compliment too highly the fashionable taste of these times, and prefer often an epigrammatical turn of wit to the sober dictates of sound criticism and religion."[14]

Carroll wanted history writing to be free from "the adulterated philosophy of present times."[15]

In 1806 Carroll, reflecting on the contestation proceeding from some German-speakers in his diocese, made a sweeping declaration on modern currents of the day that came from Germany. "You, I doubt not," he wrote to a priest, "will lament with me the corruption of principle and practice which has been effected by the diffusion of illuminism from the Protestant German universities into those of Catholics, and even into convents and religious orders."[16] The editor of the *John Carroll Papers,* Thomas O. Hanley, in a footnote links Carroll's term *illuminism* with the Illuminati of Adam Weishaupt. It seems to me, however, that Carroll, with the English-language usage of his day, was referring to a much broader school, and that he could have expressed his thought just as well with the term *enlightenment*—if *enlightened* and *enlightenment* had been in his commonly used vocabulary.[17]

Carroll's generally negative view of the Enlightenment can be observed in his characterization of some individuals usually associated with the Enlightenment.

For example, he calls Abbé Guillaume Raynal "an enthusiast, I had almost said the Bedlamite of liberty."[18]

Another example is found in Carroll's references to Emperor Joseph II, 1741–1790, a leading Catholic figure of the Enlightenment. Carroll disagreed with "the fashionable language of extolling the Emperor as a model of princes . . . the so much admired Joseph." In Carroll's view, Joseph II was one more example of a "despotical tyrant."[19] In 1790, before sailing to England, Carroll wrote his friend Charles Plowden that "the Emperor's character is viewed here as opprobrious and paltry in the extreme."[20] Carroll denounced Father John Goetz and suspended him from the ministry on several counts, including Josephinism and other Enlightenment currents.[21] Ten years later Carroll judged that part of the problem with Goetz was that he had been trained in "the principles of the late Emperor Joseph."[22]

When the Court of Spain was at a high tide of Enlightenment (1782), Carroll, still smarting from Charles III's action against the Society of Jesus, referred to "that obstinate and still more ignorant government."[23]

Charles Wharton, a friend and relation of Carroll, stopped serving as a priest, left the Church and published an anti-Catholic pamphlet. When Carroll first learned of Wharton's disaffection, he described him as "*un peu philosophe,* but I hope not too much so."[24] Subsequently, after Wharton's book, Carroll recognized he had been too optimistic in his earlier assessment of Wharton's "more liberal view."[25]

Carroll found traditional ideas and ways fairly congenial, as did most of his Maryland-born ex-Jesuit brethren. Although he was more enterprising than they were, he did not connaturally esteem the "modern" of his day. Yet his mind was open to wide-ranging contacts, and he did not want to be as close-minded as some he knew. Nevertheless, at times he drew the line. For example, when the archbishop of Mainz offered to provide gratis in his seminary for some young American students, Carroll, poor as he was and in need of trained American-born priests, hesitated because, after his experience with John Charles Heilbron, he did not like those "incongruous doctrines on the authority of the laity, particularly in some German universities." He waited so that first he could inquire (in Rome) about the theology taught in Mainz.[26]

Carroll was a "rational" thinker, but his "rationalism" was that of scholastic philosophy, of the Thomist species that valued intellect in the face of other species that emphasized will. The harmony between nature and grace, which some commentators find in Carroll, probably proceeds from this same source. In the Thomist School's teaching, "grace builds on nature." Similarly the reasonable apologetics of Carroll antedates the Enlightenment. In Carroll's own view of the forming of his mind it was the "college" that had left its mark. Presumably he meant not only St. Omers, where he studied as a youth, but also the novitiate at Wappen and his Jesuit seminary education at Liége. To my knowledge, no biographer has found, in what Carroll wrote or what others wrote about him, any critical point in his life where he changed the matrix of his thought and gave up the "moderate rationalism" of the scholasticism he had learned. In the correspondence of Carroll one does not find many quotations of authors, but what few there are touch usually upon Church affairs, and so are quotations drawn from ecclesiastics rather than philosophers and *literati*. In his self-consciousness Carroll sensed he was rather conservative in comparison even with some currents within the Church; this he expressed to his confidant Charles Plowden.[27] Carroll's correspondence with those who challenged his authority shows that he was a rational thinker also in the sense that he was able to overcome his feelings in a conflict and with charity achieve reconciliation for the common good.

2. Liberty, democracy and revolution.

Carroll favored liberty, and by the American Revolution had become a republican.[28] Yet, by and large, his views were center-of-the-road, with a slight edge toward the conservative. He sided with the Federalists rather than with the Democratic Republicans. Carroll mistrusted in Church or State what he referred to—toward the end of his life—as "furious democracy."[29] In his long-term view he felt that many cited "the rights of the people" as a cover for their hidden agenda.[30] In an era of violent revolution he praised the peaceful restraint of the Catholic population of Ireland when it asked for an end to discrimination, discrimination which the Bishop of Baltimore agreed was evil and should be ended.[31] But he did not want the end of it to come via revolution *à la française;* he did not want to see the destruction of the government and constitution of England.[32]

When Carroll looked at the French Revolution, he found himself in basic agreement with Edmund Burke's *Reflections on the French Revolution,* but he found Burke too smug in regard to English policy and the fairness of representation in the British parliament.[33] In 1790, even before the revolution in France turned violent, Carroll decried its "gripping hand of irreligious despotism."[34] Precisely because Carroll favored greater liberty in France, he could not accept certain provisions imposed by the new regime, for example, the Civil Constitution of the Clergy.[35]

Toward the end of the decade Carroll was using sterner language; the horrors of war and persecution, he judged, had by 1798 led the European populace, "so long stunned with the empty noise of liberty and equality, [to] know now the full value of those words in the mouth of modern Frenchman [sic]."[36]

One idea that was anathema to Carroll was the proposal that at least in a democratic republic the parish priest/pastor should be elected by the local congregation.[37] Carroll insisted, on the contrary, that the appointment was the prerogative of the bishop, who had to judge the credentials and fitness of the candidate. The right of patronage, which had been exercised in other lands and places, had not entered the United States of America; since Catholic church buildings in the USA had contributors who lived far away, and contributors who were not Catholics, Carroll argued that the *jus patronatus* logic was defective and did not apply.[38]

On the other hand, Carroll was willing to cooperate with boards of trustees to whom was committed the corporate ownership and management of church property. Such lay responsibility fit in with his distinction between the spiritual role of the bishop and the temporal administration of properties. His stance in this matter was not drawn from Enlightenment ideas. In the states of the United States the Catholic Church like other religious bodies had to form a civil corporation which, as a corporate person, would be the owner of the property. Without such a corporation the only possible arrangement was ownership in the name of individuals. Thus the ownership by a board was a matter of the civil law on property; it was not an option based on religious philosophy. In the western part of his diocese, in the former French colonial towns in the Northwest Territory, lay boards had been created according to French ecclesiastical law, which had developed long before the Enlightenment era.[39] Thus, while insisting on his episcopal authority to appoint the parish priest, Carroll was ready to cooperate with lay management and popular participation according to any legal structure present in the diocese.

In summary, then, Carroll appears as a moderately convervative republican, whose political-theory heritage is that of centuries of European tradition in regard to limited government: medieval contractualism, Thomas Aquinas, Robert Bellarmine, Francisco Suárez, and also the English jurists of the fifteenth century followed by the authors of the Revolution of 1688. From these sources Carroll could form his personal rights-of-man philosophy and constitutionalism without eighteenth-century authors. By his continental-European education and by keeping up on the news, Carroll was aware of Enlightenment-era or French-Revolutionary positions but did not take to them.

3. "Enlightened despotism," with an ecclesiastical policy associated with Joseph II or with Justinus Febronius, pseudonym of Johann Nikolaus von Hontheim (1701–1790).

"Febronianism" would be a litmus test for Catholic Enlightenment: how far would one go in conceding to the State control over the Catholic Church within its domain? "Josephinist" or "Febronian" political figures and authors sought a sort of national Catholic Church that would resemble the model Henry VIII provided for England, but without rupture from Rome unless Rome should take ill-advised actions.

We have seen above how Carroll characterized Joseph II, who was a paladin of Catholic Enlightenment.

The American federal union, towards which Carroll was devoutly patriotic, acknowledged that it should abstain from legislation in ecclesiastical matters. Carroll's position was practically identical with the First Amendment of the United States Constitution of 1787, ratified in 1789, which provided that the government should not legislate concerning the establishment of a Church or impede the free exercise of religion. In 1790 he joined in an address to President George Washington which hoped for the end of the restrictions that still remained in a few states in regard to Catholics.[40] Thus the thought of John Carroll, opposed to all state control over religious affairs, was anti-Febronian.

Carroll was, however, careful not to participate in the English Catholics' debates, while he followed them closely, for example the debates over the naming of bishops and over proposed formulas of an oath to be taken by Catholic subjects. Although John Milner militantly opposed allowing the royal government any control over the naming of bishops, Carroll felt that a veto could conceivably be granted.[41] In a sense, Carroll had gone along with an American federal government veto when he relayed to Rome the negative wishes of the United States government in regard to the choosing of a bishop for the see of New Orleans.[42]

After the vicars apostolic of England had pronounced their judgment on the formula proposed to be required of Catholic subjects, Carroll privately agreed, saying how degrading he found the government's terms. He felt that some Catholics were willing to cede too much to the government in accepting humiliating, indeed quasi-calumnious expressions.[43]

In the United States Carroll opposed the 1786 oath required by New York State, because it was anti-papal.[44] In
his diocese he had a right and duty to speak that in the
British struggle for Catholic Emancipation he did not have.

In the balance, Carroll comes off as anti-Febronian; his
position is quite distant from that of the Catholic Enlightenment figures. However well intentioned were the reformers, and however real were their reforms, they were determined to promote an efficient, tight, centralized control.
They were an elite replacing another elite, they were not
freedom-promoting democrats. Their statecraft, involving
rigid regalism, was far from the political philosophy of the
Marylander.

4. Gallicanism. In countries other than France, a similar
phenomenon existed without the name, that is, an equiva-
lent stance of episcopal authority vis-à-vis Roman authority. A Spanish historian calls it *episcopalismo anticurial*.[45]
Carroll's correspondence with Rome does not evidence
"anti-curial episcopalism." (His attitude toward the Holy
See is further treated below in Heading Number 7.) The
position he developed on the choosing of bishops sought no
more of Rome than was common for diocesan chapters.

In 1790 Carroll feared what the American government
leaders might make of the words "for this time only" in the
bull that established the diocese in the United States and
permitted election of the bishop by the clergy "for this time
only."[46] Ironically the United States government's intervention came not in regard to the dioceses subsequently
created in 1808 but rather in regard to New Orleans, and
John Carroll was the government's intermediary; the
bishop of Baltimore acted to exclude one who might have
been elected by the local clergy.[47] So the first bishop of
Baltimore reaffirmed (1790) his view that future American
bishops should be elected as he had been,—except that in
the future, with the growth of the clergy, new members,

who, of course, had not been members of the Society of Jesus, should participate in the electing chapter.[48] In the event, though, when Carroll chose his coadjutor and when the four dioceses were created in 1808, he did not organize elections but he did consult. He was the first and last bishop chosen in the United States by an electoral body made up of all the clergy.

In 1793 Carroll asked for authorization to form a cathedral chapter in his diocese, made up of the "more respectable" pastors, which would govern the diocese *sede vacante;* the pope "benignly accorded this."[49] The Baltimore chapter, though, did not materialize. If Carroll was aware that the pope had approved his proposal, the reason why he did not go ahead may be connected with the absence, preferred by Carroll and permitted by Rome, of canonically established pastors in the diocese. (Even as late as 1866 the bishops of the Second Plenary Council of Baltimore decided that this departure from normal canon law should continue because the time was not yet ripe for conforming to the norm.[50] In the post-Carroll era groups of archbishops or bishops or diocesan consultors prepared *ternae,* but the precise mode of 1789 was never repeated, nor were real chapters created.) The reasons for Carroll's policy cannot be pursued here, but the absence of the diocesan chapter was not due to Roman opposition.

On one particular point Carroll was very strong: the Church in the United States was mature after a century and a half of life, and was not to be considered a mission; therefore, he argued, it should not lie under the jurisdiction of the Congregation de Propaganda Fide; nevertheless for a quarter of a century Bishop Carroll corresponded placidly and effectively with Propaganda Fide. Meanwhile Rome tolerated the sign of a not-yet-mature situation described in the previous paragraph. (See also Heading Number 7 below.)

Carroll was willing to admit for France free theological

discussion of the Gallican articles until final settlement by the Church.[51] But he made bluntly clear to Henri Grégoire his disagreement with the "constitutional" bishop's ideas, which were partly Gallican and partly Febronian.[52] Carroll frankly chided Grégoire for insufficiently upholding the Holy See and for quoting frequently from a Gallican-Jansenist anthology that was notoriously unreliable.[53]

5. Apology for Jansenism,—with a positive attitude toward the Synod of Pistoia and a negative attitude toward the Society of Jesus and the devotion to the Sacred Heart of Jesus.

John Carroll had suffered in seeing the dissolution of the Society of Jesus in France, where the Jansenists had been the most efficient antagonists, and in seeing the suppression of the Society in the Church at large, thanks in part to Jansenist pamphleteering. (Jansenists' presence in the ranks of the Catholic Enlightenment was paradoxical, for they represented rigid, dogmatic doctrines regarding redemption and moral theology, doctrines which were the antithesis of the Age of Reason.) Assuredly, then, Carroll had no soft spot in his heart for this wing or aspect of the "Catholic Enlightenment."

Carroll stood by Roman decrees against Jansenism.[54] In contending with Father Caesarius Reuter in Philadelphia Carroll had occasion to recall the papal condemnation of the Synod of Pistoia.[55]

Regarding the devotion to the Sacred Heart of Jesus, Carroll sought for the Baltimore diocese whatever Rome was granting elsewhere. He informed Propaganda Fide that there was much devotion to the Sacred Heart in his diocese.[56] Carroll's mind was far from that of the "enlightened" group who denounced the "heart-worshipers."[57]

6. Religious tolerance.

John Carroll fully favored civil tolerance in religious

affairs. This tenet the Catholic Enlightenment also shared, with exception made for Febronian limitations. Europe, though, had other and earlier sources to consult in favor of tolerance.[58] In theology, however, Carroll was unyielding. His civil tolerance did not engender a theological tolerance. What he termed "theological intolerance" he considered to be· "essential to true religion."[59] His "Address to the Roman Catholics of the United States of America by a Catholic Clergyman" (1784) sets forth at length the uniqueness of the Catholic Church and its traditions.[60]

Asked whether the Church of England had apostolic succession, Carroll answered negatively and gave his reasons.[61]

Carroll had no difficulty at all with William DuBourg's school in Baltimore where Catholic pupils were outnumbered by Protestants (1808).[62] But the use of a Catholic church building by Protestants was a different matter.[63] Whenever he saw that a relative of his might marry a non-Catholic, Carroll was uneasy.[64]

Within the Catholic Church he was not pleased with some of the discussions he heard about. He reacted with dismay when he learned that some Catholic priests in England were in favor of abolishing the requirement of celibacy of the clergy; he hoped they were few.[65]

He was at first overjoyed that Joseph Berington, an English Catholic priest who moved in Catholic Enlightenment currents, had written on tolerance. But then, judging that Berington gave away what had to maintained, Carroll saw how much they disagreed.[66]

Carroll's theology is cut from the cloth of the continental scholasticism he studied at Liége, without any signs of Enlightenment threads; nor for that matter does he weave in any particularly American trends of thought, except in the matter of civil tolerance. As early as 1634 Maryland had known tolerance, but later lost it. The question of intolerance had been such an issue in Carroll's family that some, not long before the American Revolution, had thought of leaving Maryland for Louisiana. So it is more reasonable to situate the origin of Carroll's position on civil toleration in his native Maryland rather than seek it in some European Enlightenment authors.

7. Expressions—beyond 4 and 5—of anti-Roman feeling.

A degree of defiance of Roman ecclesiastical authority was a typical characteristic of "Enlightenment Catholicism" whether it was along the lines of a churchman like Bishop Scipione de' Ricci in the diocese of Pistoia or along the lines of government ministers in royal or princely courts.

On the level of experience and perception John Carroll had been shaken by what he saw in Rome during the months of his sojourn there from October 1772 to June 1773. On the doctrinal level he wished (1784) that some "philosophical divine" would ascertain the "extent and boundaries of the spiritual jurisdiction of the Holy See."[67] In the political order Carroll was ever concerned lest the Holy See take a step which the United States government would resent as intervention of a foreign power. And in regard to ecclesiastical property ownership Carroll had a *sui generis* notion of the division between spiritual authority and temporal possessions. In the working out of his views, however, Carroll seems to have become more Rome-oriented as the years went by; that particular evolution will not be pressed here, but only the degree to which Carroll was sensitive to anti-Roman expressions of Catholics.

In the 1770s John Carroll felt and spoke strongly about Rome. So traumatizing was Carroll's Roman visit of 1772–1773 that he could clearly recall details fifteen years later. Yet, even though he acquired a lasting low opinion of Clement XIV, he firmly disbelieved the anecdotes, published post-mortem, that charged the late pope with private misbehavior.[68]

In 1784 Carroll opined that bishops in various countries had been too slack in taking the lead to bring Rome around to accepting the use of the vernacular in the liturgy.[69] But he drew the line sharply when some in England thought he favored the change without the approbation of the Holy See.[70]

Later, Bishop, then Archbishop Carroll did not take the lead in this regard. He did, though, arrange for a hymnal with vernacular hymns that were sung at Mass; he archly said that the moments or intervals these English hymns occupied were in Italy and elsewhere filled with "symphonies, solos, or some motet, not always connected with the office of the day."[71]

The fact that the papal curia dealt with Benjamin Franklin without consulting the clergy in the new nation was for Carroll another sign of Propaganda Fide's "aversion to the remains of the Society," but at the same time he wished that no intemperate letter be sent to Rome.[72] Carroll wanted the future American bishop to be chosen within the new nation for a diocese that would be set up with ordinary jurisdiction rather than with missionary dependence on Propaganda Fide.[73] Actually, the Paris nuncio's conversations probably had no anti-Jesuit matrix and probably took place because the peace treaty was composed in Paris, because France was a Catholic ally of the United States, and because Roman diplomacy began by seeking formulas for protection of the Church as well as for creating a hierarchy. Propaganda had little knowledge of the "natives" and their clergy in North America.[74] But Carroll, familiar with the history of missions and the Chinese Rites controversy, viewed Propaganda Fide as a congregation that had "always been unfavourable to the Society."[75] He was dead set against Propaganda Fide's ever acquiring American ex-Jesuit property, which, he was careful to note, had never belonged to the Society at large, that is, to the Jesuit order as such, but rather only to specific local units.[76]

After initial hesitation Carroll accepted an offer from Propaganda Fide to educate two of his seminarians, and in 1787 the first two sailed for Europe. Diplomatically Carroll sought to know what kind of obligation the Congregation would impose on the graduates.[77]

While not forgetting history or human frailty, Carroll cooperated with Propaganda, and became increasingly pleased with the treatment he received. As the years went by, he felt that ex-Jesuits should not judge the contemporary Propaganda cardinals harshly, and dreamed of the day when a restored Society of Jesus would collaborate cordially with Propaganda Fide. His personal deference, though, was not time-serving, but proceeded from obedience to the Holy See, along with a feeling that persons and times had changed.[78]

Not only in a Rome seminary did Carroll receive Roman alms but also in Baltimore and Georgetown, apparently without fear of what citizens or government might say about papal subsidizing of a diocese and a school in the United States. In September 1790 he implied that the contributions from Propaganda Fide had tipped the balance so that his planned academy in Georgetown could surely open.[79] The bishop received for the school a subsidy of 100 *scudi* for three years that was renewed at intervals.[80] In 1798 he expected that seminarians who along with lay students attended the college in Georgetown would learn "zeal, pure faith and inevitable fidelity to the Holy See."[81] Carroll also begged from Propaganda a steady contribution to support his fledgling diocese; in 1790 he began getting the handsome subsidy of 200 gold pieces a year.[82]

In 1790 Carroll, recently consecrated bishop, wrote that the Holy See had "just prerogatives," but in its history had known "iniquities and oppression"; the extension of what was originally rightful jurisdiction "sooner or later always does harm."[83] On the other hand, since Carroll was neither sycophant nor schizophrenic, one must not discard as cant or mood what he wrote about the same time to Cardinal Leonardo Antonelli (July 1790): "Daily experience teaches me that faith and morals are kept intact if there is a close union with Christ's vicar on earth, and that nearly every lapse in either originates in a diminution of respect for the See of Peter."[84]

As of 1786 Carroll began telling of his displeasure with the attitude of his English priest friend Joseph Berington, who, in Carroll's view, had gone too far in limiting Roman prerogatives. More firmly in 1795 Carroll rejected "that disrespect, I almost said hatred, which Mr. Joseph Berington's late works endeavour to infuse against the Holy See."[85]

To the parishioners of Holy Trinity Church in Philadelphia the bishop of Baltimore in 1797 gave a vibrant explanation of the meaning of communion with Rome, and he tied his episcopal authority to the See of Peter.[86] Seventeen years later, when Pius VII, released from captivity, returned to Rome (24 May 1814) after a long, slow journey, Archbishop Carroll issued a vigorous pastoral letter (7 July 1814) full of warmth and joy. Here the sentiments of the mature Carroll vis-à-vis pope and Holy See are manifested.[87] As the "Cisalpines" were evolving in England, Carroll was proving "ultramontane."

During the course of his episcopate Carroll accepted and fostered the devotions and piety of his diocese. He pursued, obtained and promulgated the papal jubilee of 1775 (in 1784) and the jubilee for the turn of century and the papal election. From the pope he sought various other indulgences. He obtained delegation for blessing rosaries. In 1808 he and his new suffragans asked and received, with authorization to delegate, the giving of the papal blessing "at the hour of death" *(in articulo mortis)*.[88] When one considers the difficulty of communication with Rome, in comparison, say, with the steamship era decades later, the Rome-related piety of the Carroll era is all the more noteworthy.

The quotations from Carroll's letters and the actions he took show that on this characteristic point of attitude-toward-Rome he was the opposite of an "Enlightenment Catholic."

Since it has been suggested that in the mature John Carroll a residual anti-Roman feeling kept him from re-entering the restored Society of Jesus, let us give full attention to this final question. In the 1790s Carroll favored papal restoration of the Society of Jesus, but he wanted the Society to be integrally what it had been before. In addition to the legal status in the worldwide Church, his understanding of a full restoration included having a superior general residing in Rome near the pope. In the first decade of the 1800s he cooperated with the step-by-step revival of the order, but he looked to a firmer juridical foundation than was then available.[89] Carroll stated in 1808 that his conscience was at stake, for when he read the rigor of Clement XIV's brief of suppression, he as bishop felt constrained in regard to the reborn Jesuits until the pope should promulgate a full, public restoration.[90]

The complete restoration that he desired came only in September 1814. In December of 1814 he learned of Pius VII's bull by way of England. By that time he was 79 years of age and could work only a few hours a day. In the spring of 1815 Carroll affirmed that he had received no direct communication from pope or curia cardinals since the beginning of the pope's confinement by Napoleon in 1809; shortly after writing that statement he got one letter from Rome.[91] The dramatic but brief return of Napoleon from Elba prolonged the interruption of communications. Thus Carroll came to the end of his life on 3 December 1815 without having had the possibility of rejoining the fully restored Society of Jesus.

Even if he had received the authenticated bull of restoration, even if health had permitted him to act, his conscience might never have permitted him to return to the Society of Jesus. Carroll had several concerns that urged him to be cautious. For example, he wondered what the reaction of American government authorities would be.[92] Then too he was unclear about whether his reentry into the Society should coincide with resigning his see, and he doubted that the pope would permit him to resign. Moreover, he thought that the Society was better off dealing with him rather than with another as archbishop during these restoration steps.[93]

All of these factors were too much for a man who repeatedly recalled that he was 80 years old. His weary head and frame had other tasks more urgent to attend to than discussing whether and how to rejoin the renascent Society. In any case, nothing in the extant documentation allows one to conclude that any anti-Roman sentiment constituted an obstacle.

CONCLUSION

In conclusion, it seems that John Carroll can hardly be linked with the Enlightenment either in the sense in which the term *Enlightenment* is used in general historiography or in the sense in which the term is used in application to some late-eighteenth-century Catholic currents, for even with a bit of bending the concepts are not Carroll's. One can, of course, usefully point out that he lived during the period of the Enlightenment, and was aware of the views that circulated in Europe and America. It is, though, also useful to add that in his sermons he preached against Enlightenment-era ideas that were anti-Christian, and in his correspondence he disagreed with the trends that were characteristic of the ''Enlightenment Catholics.''

Carroll was a "man of his times," but, neither *avant-garde* nor a mossback, was discerning in what he took from his times. What he did find congenial he more probably first drew from intellectual fonts not precisely connected with the Enlightenment. The image, circulated during the 1980s, of a John Carroll concordant with the currents of illuminism and the Age of Reason does not fit the picture he limned of himself in the letters, sermons and documents he authored. John Carroll was a reasonable, kind, wise, intelligent, dutiful bishop, and he was an urbane, tolerant, moderate, liberty-loving republican. Nonetheless,—if he could arise to join the discussion, he might, in the way he revised his own letters, scratch out that word "nonetheless" and write "therefore"—John Carroll was not an "Enlightenment bishop."

Notes

1. *The English Catholic Enlightenment. John Lingard and the Cisalpine Movement 1780–1850,* Shepardstown, 1980.

2. "Aufklärung," I (Freiburg, 1957) 1059–1062.

3. Chiara d'Afflitto, "Cenni biografici su Scipione de' Ricci," *Scipione de' Ricci e la realtà pistoiese della fine del settecento* (Pistoia, 1986), p. 9.

4. *Théologie et politique au siècle des lumières (1770–1820),* (Genève, 1973), pp. 317–318. Also Bernard Plongeron, "L'Aufklärung Catholique en Europe Occidentale de 1770 à 1830. Essai de définition," *Bulletin de la Société d'Histoire Moderne,* supplément à la *Revue d'Histoire Moderne et Contemporaine,* 14ème série, No. 10, pp. 13–16, séance du 2 mars 1969.

5. "Religion, séparation et libertés, de l'ancien régime à la Révolution," *Etudes* 371 (1989) 213–233.

6. "La religiosidad de los ilustrados," in *Historia de España,* (Madrid, 1987), Miguel Batllori et al., XXXI/1, *La época de Ilustración,* p. 398.

7. "La 'Ilustración' y el destierro de la Compañía de Jesús" in *La Compañía de Jesús en Alcala de Henares (1546–1989)* (Alcalá, 1989), especially 57–66.

8. *Oxford English Dictionary* (Oxford, 1978), II, 439.

9. "An Eighteenth-Century Bishop: John Carroll of Baltimore," *Archivum Historiae Pontificiae* 16 (1978) 171–204.

10. "Address to the Roman Catholics of the United States. . . ," 1784, *John Carroll Papers,* ed. Thomas O. Hanley, (3 vols. Notre Dame, 1976), [hereafter = JCP], 1, 140.

11. Carroll to Plowden, 23 October 1789, JCP, 1, 389.

12. For example, Carroll to Charles Plowden, 12 February 1803, JCP, 2, 409.

13. Carroll to Troy, 22 June 1795, JCP, 2, 143.

14. Carroll to Robert Plowden, 2 March 1798, JCP, 2, 232.

15. Carroll to Charles Plowden, 7 March 1798, JCP 2, 234.

16. Carroll to [William Elling], 17 August 1806, JCP, 2, 527.

17. See *illuminism* in *Oxford English Dictionary* (Oxford, 1978) V, 48.

18. Carroll to Charles Plowden, 20 February 1782, JCP 1, 67.

19. Carroll to Charles Plowden, 20 February 1782, JCP, 1, 78–79.

20. 16 March 1790, JCP, 1, 434.

21. Carroll to William O'Brien, 8 November [1787], JCP, 1, 268.

22. Carroll to Robert Plowden, 7 July 1797, JCP, 2, 219.

23. Carroll to Charles Plowden, 20 February 1782, JCP, 1, 79.

24. Carroll to Charles Plowden, 10 April 1784, JCP, 1, 147.

25. Carroll to Charles Plowden, 27 February 1785, JCP, 1, 167.

26. Carroll to Antonelli, July 1790, JCP, 1, 446–448.

27. 27 February 1785, JCP, 1, 167.

28. JCP, 1, 65.

29. Carroll to Charles Plowden, 25 June-24 July 1815, JCP, 3, 339.

30. *Ibid.*

31. Carroll to Troy, 22 June 1795 and 21 March 1810, JCP, 2, 143; 3, 115. Carroll to Charles Plowden, 7 July 1797, JCP, 2, 217.

32. Carroll to Charles Plowden, 12 October 1791, JCP, 1, 523.

33. Carroll to Charles Plowden, 3 February and 21 March 1791, JCP, 1, 492 and 500–501.

34. Carroll to Charles Plowden, 25 September 1790, JCP, 1, 466.

35. Carroll to Zacharie and Latil, 2 December 1791, JCP, 1, 546–547.

36. Carroll to Charles Plowden, 13 December 1798, JCP 2, 250.

37. JCP 1, 311, 382–383, 387.

38. JCP, 1, 391, 426.

39. Carroll to Administrators of Vincennes, 19 October 1796, Carroll to the Congregation of Raisin River, 19 October 1796, JCP 2, 190–192. On French law regarding *marguilliers* or *fabriciens* see Louis Héricourt, *Les Loix Ecclésiastiques de France,* p. 656 in the Paris edition of 1756.

40. JCP, 1, 410.

41. JCP, 3, 241, 312, 330, 341–341, 352.

42. Charles E. O'Neill, " 'A Quarter Marked by Sundry Peculiarities': New Orleans, Lay Trustees and Père Antoine," *Catholic Historical Review* 76 (1990), 235–277.

43. JCP 1, 432, 472, 474, 491; 2, 121.

44. Carroll to Nugent, 18 July 1786, JCP, 1, 215.

45. Teófanes Egido, a "La religiosidad de los ilustrados," in *Historia de España*, (Madrid, Espasa-Calpe, 1987), Miguel Batllori et al., XXXI/1, *La época de Ilustración*, p. 408.

46. Carroll to Charles Plowden, 2 September 1790, JCP, 1, 455.

47. O'Neill, *Catholic Historical Review*, 76 (1990), 235–277.

48. Carroll to Ashton, 18 April 1790, JCP 1, 436.

49. Rome, Archivio della Congregazione de Propaganda Fide, Acta 1793, vol. 163, f. 463.

50. *Concilii Plenarii Baltimorensis II*. . . . *Acta et Decreta* (Baltimore, 1894), p. 79, decree paragraph 123.

51. Carroll to Garnier, 31 August 1809, JCP, 3, 95.

52. 9 September 1809, JCP, 3, 105.

53. 4 June 1811, JCP, 3, 150.

54. Carroll to Garnier, 29 April 1806, JCP, 2, 512.

55. Carroll to Brancadoro, 12 October 1799, JCP, 2, 287.

56. JCP, 1, 27; 2, 375, 434. Rome, Archivio della Congregazione de Propaganda Fide, Acta, 1793, vol. 163, f. 464.

57. Scipione de Ricci, "Istruzione pastorale di Monsig. Vescovo sulla nuova devozione al Cuor di Gesù," *Atti e decreti del Concilio Diocesano di Pistoia dell'anno 1786* (2 vols. Florence, 1986), I, 95. Paintings of unknown artist depicting in unfavorable light Jesuits and devotion to the Sacred Heart of Jesus in *Scipione de' Ricci e la realtà pistoiese della fine del settecento* (Pistoia, 1986), pp. 194–198.

58. Joseph Lecler, *Histoire de la tolérance au siècle de la réforme*, 2 vols. Paris, 1955.

59. Carroll to Troy, 12 July 1794, JCP, 2, 121.

60. JCP, 1, 82–144.

61. [1790] JCP, 1, 414–416.

62. JCP, 3, 37.

63. Carroll to William Vousdan, 10 September 1801, JCP, 2, 362.

64. JCP 1, 275; 2, 514; 3, 92.

65. Carroll to Charles Plowden, 4 June 1787, JCP, 1, 253. Carroll to [Coghlan], 13 June 1787, JCP 1, 255.

66. Carroll to Berington, 10 July 1784, JCP, 1, 148. Carroll to Charles Plowden, 23 May 1796, 2, 178–179.

67. Carroll to Berington, 1784, JCP, 1, 148.

68. JCP, 1, 26–30, 192, 224–225 198, 221, 245, 475.

69. Carroll to Berington, 10 July 1784, JCP 1, 149. Carroll's view antedated the wish expressed by the Synod of Pistoia, *Atti e decreti del Concilio Diocesano di Pistoia dell'anno 1786,* reprinted in Florence, 1986, p. 131.

70. Carroll to Charles Plowden, 4 June 1787, JCP 1, 253.

71. Carroll to Troy, 22 June 1795, JCP, 1, 143.

72. Carroll to Charles Plowden, 18 September 1784, JCP 1, 151.

73. JCP 1, 146, 156, 162–166. 241, 280, 298.

74. Charles E. O'Neill, "The United States of America," in *Sacrae Congregationis de Propaganda Fide Memoria Rerum,* II, 1700–1815 (Rome/Freiburg/Wien, 1972), p. 1166.

75. Carroll to the Gentlemen of the Southern District, [1787], JCP, 1, 227.

76. JCP 1, 227 and 475.

77. JCP 1, 153, 164, 173, 187, 216, 236, 255, 356.

78. JCP 1, 282, 199, 319, 357, 359, 428; 3, 87, 141, 160, 292.

79. Carroll to Antonelli, 27 September 1790, JCP 1, 467.

80. Rome, Archivio della Congregazione de Propaganda Fide, Acta, 1788, vol. 158, f. 2; 1789, vol. 159, f. 249; 1792, vol. 162, f. 143. Udienze, 1805, f. 324. *United States Documents in the Propaganda Fide Archives. A Calendar,* Finbar Kenneally, ed., (Washington, 1966–) 3, 214–215.

81. Carroll to Robert Plowden, 2 March 1798, JCP 2, 233.

82. JCP 1, 448. Even though Carroll often spoke of his apprehension over "foreign" hands in the Church in America, he overcame that concern and also his patriotic antipathy when he begged Napoleon to send a contribution for the construction of the Baltimore cathedral. After all the First Consul had just sold Louisiana to the Americans! Carroll to Bonaparte, 26 August 1803, JCP 2, 424. Similarly, however he felt about the Court of Charles III and Charles IV, he was grateful for the Spanish gift for a church in his diocese. Carroll to Viar, 20 April 1790, JCP 1, 437.

83. Carroll to Charles Plowden, 4 October 1790, JCP 1, 475.

84. JCP 1, 447.

85. Carroll to Charles Plowden, 13 November 1795, JCP 1, 157. Also JCP 1, 218, 220, 225; 2, 157.

86. JCP 2, 202–203.

87. JCP 3, 279–283.

88. Rome, Archivio della Congregazione de Propaganda Fide, Udienze 1784, ff. 246v–247; 1807, f. 259; 1808, f. 339.

89. Carroll 2, 132–134, 446–447, 483, 494, 512; 3, 36, 47, 50, 121, 141, 237, 253, 255.

90. JCP 1, 319; 3, 47, 247, 250, 324.

91. JCP 3, 314, 325–330, 362.

92. Carroll to Charles Plowden, 5 January 1815, JCP 3, 317.

93. JCP 3, 317.

The Eucharist as Presented in the Corpus Christi Sermons of Colonial Anglo-America

Joseph C. Linck

For the small and scattered Catholic community of Anglo-colonial America in the mid-to-late eighteenth century,
a great deal of importance was attached to the sermons
which they heard delivered during Mass. Lacking both
access to regularly offered religious instruction—which
would in a later century be available through a private
school system—and a network of established parishes, they
looked to the often-times sporadic visits of missionary
priests to fulfill this educational role. Thus it was the task
of the missionary preacher to deliver sermons that would
both inform and inspire, exhort and reprove. An examination of these homilies can provide the researcher with
valuable insights into the piety and beliefs of the Catholics
of that time and place. This paper will take as its particular
subject the catechesis that was offered concerning the
Eucharist: both the way the Sacrament was presented in
and of itself, and the role it was seen to play in the life of
the faithful Catholic Christian, through a study of seven
sermons delivered in commemoration of the feast of Corpus
Christi from 1762 through the end of the century.[1] These
sermons are included in the "American Catholic Sermon

Collection" housed in the Special Collections of Georgetown University's Lauinger Library; the collection consists
of sermons taken from the Archives of Woodstock College,
the Maryland Jesuit Province, and Georgetown University
itself. Six preachers are responsible for the sermons treated
in this paper: John Bolton (d.1809), John-Baptist Diderich
(d.1793), James Frambach (d.1795), Henry Pile (d.1813),
Louis Roels (d.1794), and Charles Sewall (d.1805), all of
whom were members of the Society of Jesus before its
suppression in 1773, and who continued to carry out their
pastoral duties even after this event. Three of these men
were born in the colonies (Bolton, Pile, and Sewall), while
the other three were originally from Europe: Diderich was
from Luxembourg, Frambach from Germany, and Roels
from Belgium.

It should be noted that while the Collection referred to
above contains other sermons that deal with the Eucharist
(e.g. sermons for First Communion), these were not included in order that this paper could focus on sermons
delivered at a particular, identifiable time in the liturgical
year, thus allowing for a greater ease in comparison and
contrast. Though limited in number, the sermons provide a
rich variety of thoughts on the Eucharist which, though
they may at times appear contradictory, actually comple-
ment each other and provide a depth that a more homoge-
neous set of sources would lack. It is the comprehensive-
ness of exposition displayed by these colonial preachers
that this paper will investigate, presenting first an analysis
of relevant passages from the sermons, followed by conclu-
sions drawn from the data.

All of the sermons consulted in the preparation of this
paper were delivered during the octave of the feast of
Corpus Christi; that is, either on the actual day of the feast,
which at the time these sermons were delivered was celebrated on the second Thursday after Pentecost Sunday, or
on the Sunday which followed it. The feast itself was

established by Pope Urban IV in 1264—who commissioned St. Thomas Aquinas to compose the texts for the Divine Office and Mass of the day—and it became quite popular after Pope Clement V issued a bull of his own on the subject in 1314, whereupon it spread throughout the Latin Church. The custom of carrying the Blessed Sacrament in procession soon became a part of the rites of the day, and a variety of pageants and customs honoring the Eucharist grew up among the various cultures of Europe. As shall become clear in the course of this paper, the feast was observed among the Catholics of Anglo-colonial America, and while they were not at liberty to conduct the more elaborate processions of their co-religionists in French and Spanish colonial America,[2] the concept of such a procession was not unknown among them.

A preparatory word must also be said concerning the liturgical texts that were used for the feast. The Epistle for the day was taken from I Corinthians 11:23–29 ("I received of the Lord, that which also I delivered to you. . . .") which contained the words used by Jesus Christ in the institution of the Eucharist ("Take and eat, this is my body. . . ."), words often quoted by the homilists, including one who uses it as his text.[3] The Gospel passage is taken from the sixth chapter of St. John, verses 56–59 ("My flesh is meat indeed, and my blood is drink indeed. . . ."). Three of the homilists chose their text from this passage.[4] Two other sermons examined in this paper take their text from the fourteenth chapter of Luke's Gospel, indicating either that they were delivered on the Sunday within the octave of Corpus Christi, for which the Gospel indicated was Luke 14:16–24 ("A man was giving a great dinner and he invited many. . . .")[5] or that they took their text from the Gospel of that day. The seventh sermon offers as its text both a passage from John 6, and one from Luke 14, indicating an admirable versatility.

When these faithful Catholics attended Mass on the feast

of Corpus Christi, what was it exactly they heard preached
to them about the Eucharist? One fundamental assertion of
every homily considered in this study is the real presence
of Christ in the Eucharist, and while none of the sermons
is devoted exclusively to an exposition of this doctrine, yet
all of the preachers deem it worthy of mention, some more
forcefully then others. Charles Sewall notes in the beginning of his sermon ". . . nor is it my design to prove in this
discourse the real presence of the body and blood of Jesus
Christ under the appearances of bread and wine . . . [this
subject] I reserve for another occasion."[6] Henry Pile, beginning his treatment of the various aspects of the Eucharist, observes ". . . for in the Blessed Eucharist is contained
really the true body and blood, soul and divinity of our
Saviour Jesus Christ under the appearance of bread and the
same under the appearance of wine. . . ."[7] Worthy of note
is the fact that both of the priests referred to above mention
the dispute over *"Utraquism"*, that is, the belief held by
certain Protestant sects that the faithful must consume both
species of the Eucharist in order to receive the fullness of
Jesus Christ and attain salvation. Pile, in addition to allud-
ing to this in his above assertion that the divinity of Christ
is present under the appearance of both bread and wine
(and not somehow split between them), further notes that
". . . the priest, tho' he receives under both kinds, receives
no more than the layman, who only receives under one
kind."[8] And Sewall, just before the passage noted above,
states that "He [Christ] does not command us to receive
under both forms, as hereticks falsely interpret those holy
words [Jn 6:54]. . . ."[9] Yet even though both refer to the
controversy, neither chooses to engage in a defense of the
practise, suggesting that, while such objections were not
unknown at the time, they were not so prevalent or dangerous as to require an extended defense.

Others among our sample of preachers, however, choose
to make a spirited defense of the doctrine of the real

presence itself, among them James Frambach. In the opening paragraphs of his sermon he makes what might be
termed a perfunctory assertion that ". . . the Holy Eucharist . . . contains the real body and blood of Jesus Christ."[10]
He continues, however, in a more impassioned vein:

> This real presence of Christ in the Blessed Sacrament
> we must believe, because we learn it from the express
> words of truth itself, so often repeated in holy Scrip-
> ture. We learn it from the express declaration of the
> Church of God, against which the gates of hell can
> never prevail. Christ himself has sayd: "This is my
> body and blood." (Mt. 26) Which words are explained
> by the common opinion of the Catholick church in a
> true sense; that Christ has given truly and realy his
> body and blood to his Apostles at the Last Supper,
> and that Christ gives us daily the same blood and body
> in the Blessed Sacrament.[11]

Here we see Frambach pursuing two lines of defense, one
based on Scripture, the other on the authority of the
Church; the former being a common approach taken by the
preachers studied in this paper. Frambach stresses that the
words of the Scriptures are clear in this matter, as Christ
himself has proclaimed "This is my body." Benjamin Roels
makes much the same point, noting that ". . . Jesus took
bread into his venerable hands, raising his eyes to heaven,
he presented it to his apostles, saying to them 'Eat, this is
my Body'. . . ."[12] John Bolton likewise notes that Jesus
proclaimed " 'My flesh is meat indeed.' "[13] John Diderich
adds a polemical flavor to the exposition when he observes
to his congregation that a great number of non-Catholic
Christians accept the real presence of Christ in the Eucharist, including

. . . their very chief reformer Luther himself, who has expressly left in his writings that he would gladly oppose the doctrine of the Eucharist, but the Scripture was so very clear on that head, that he knew not how to go about to deny it. Thus vanishes the invincible difficulty of our adversaries who either refuse to see the truth in this point, or thro' partiality or prejudice are blinded, when they read clear and manifest Scriptures on this head.[14]

Thus these Catholic preachers stress the scriptural foundations of the Eucharist, using to their own advantage an authority which was often, on other topics, to be a foundation of their opponents' position. They were doubtless aware of the weight and usefulness of this line of argument for a congregation living as a minority in the midst of denominations which put great credence in the words of Scripture.

This can also be seen in the fact that Frambach alone stresses the authority of the church as an argument for the persuasiveness of the real presence—the only one of the seven to do so. All the preachers refer quite often to the witness of the early church Fathers in other questions (as shall be mentioned below), but on the question of the real presence they are inclined to employ Scripture in their defense, if they do choose to present one. This demonstrates neither an ignorance of church teaching, nor a rejection of it, but rather a realistic appreciation of the effectiveness, clarity and strength of the scriptural argument for the community which was being addressed.

There is one other defense of the real presence of Christ in the Eucharist that, while not strictly taking the form of an appeal to church authority, does invoke what the preacher calls the "testimony of the learned," against an appeal to that which is intelligible through sense experience. John Diderich informs his congregation that certain reformers claim the real presence is contrary to their senses, yet he points out that they have no difficulty accepting the fact that the sun is

> . . . of a greater size than the earth, tho' their senses seem to tell them the contrary. They also get over this difficulty in the belief of one God in three persons, which is far above the reach of human understanding and capacity. . . . The former or the belief in the sun's being of a greater magnitude than the earth, being at least a hundred thousand times bigger than the whole globe on which we dwell, this, I say, they dare not deny, because the testimony of the learned forbids them. . . .[15]

It would seem that Diderich is arguing here against a sensist perspective that places a greater emphasis on what can be known through sense experience as opposed to that which is perceived solely through faith. Yet, as he indicates, even those whó style themselves as sensists at times accept as true something of which they themselves have no tangible proof, and many of these truths contradict the testimony of their senses. It therefore can be reduced to a matter of whose testimony is to be believed, and Diderich leaves no doubt as to the strength of his witnesses, claiming that ". . . the universal testimony of the learned part of Christianity (a very small number within these two last centuries only excepted) agree in this. . . ."[16]

Once the preachers had established at the outset of their sermons the presence of Christ in the Eucharist, they then proceeded, in almost every case, to a disquisition on the manner and frequency with which the Sacrament was to be received, and the benefits that were given to a worthy communicant. In studying these orations the reader cannot help but notice that some preachers stress simultaneously two aspects of Christ's presence in the Eucharist, while others choose to dwell on only one. From these sermons one learns that the Lord is both majestic and awesome, kind and loving; though he demands purity and devotion from those who would approach to receive him, yet he desires all to communicate often, for without his aid progress in the earthly life, and entrance into the life hereafter, is well nigh impossible. Though these two over-arching themes seem at times disparate and even contradictory, a careful examination of them will show that each is seen as necessary for a proper understanding of the other by the priests who enunciate them. What has been termed the "awesome" aspect of Christ's presence in the Eucharist— that which stresses the gulf that separates man from God— will be examined first, followed by a consideration of the benefits conferred by a frequent reception of the Eucharist: its value as a source of strength for man's earthly journey, as a pledge of eternal life, and as token of Christ's love for mankind.

James Frambach is the one in whom this emphasis on the majesty of Christ's presence in the Eucharist can most clearly be seen. "O what reverence," he implores,

> . . . ought we to bring with us, when we draw near to so tremendous a Majesty, in whose sight the whole creation is a mere nothing? What fear ought we to bring, when we enter into his sanctuary, who is infinitely pure and holy, who sees all our guilt, and cannot endure iniquity.[17]

He continues by asking his listeners:

> . . . how ought we to annihilate ourselves in the sight of this great God, and Maker of heaven and earth! How ought we to fear and to tremble, with what profound reverence we ought to approach to the holy of holies, who lies here concealed under the sacramental veils![18]

The image that is presented here of the Eucharist has more than a slight flavor of the Old Testament to it. One hears echoes of the Psalms, for example, in references to Christ as the "holy of holies," "veiled" from men's eyes by the accidents of the Eucharist, and in the description of the "tremendous" God who resides in his sanctuary. Indeed, it is important to note as a fundamental assertion that these preachers believed that the Christ who was really present to them in the Eucharist was the one and the same Word who was present with God the Father in the beginning, and through whom the world was made.[19] Therefore the Eucharist was the presence of the creator of the world and the author of all life among men, and it required little rhetorical embellishment (though this did not obviate its use) to make people aware of the resultant "awesomeness" of the Sacrament. Diderich exclaims that ". . . it is unconceivable, [that] a god can condescend and humble himself so low, as he necessarily must, in order to work this miracle. . . ."[20]

Because of this majesty of God, and in thanksgiving for the fact that God has condescended to humble himself to such a great degree, by taking on flesh and suffering for the sins of the human race, Christians are urged to give to the Eucharist the adoration to which it is entitled. Indeed the sermon of John Bolton deals almost entirely with the subject of the honor which ought to be shown toward the Eucharist. He exhorts his listeners saying, "Let us, Dear Christians . . . prostrate ourselves in his sacred presence and there offer him a thousand sacrifices of praise, of interior adoration and thanksgiving. . . ."[21] Quoting St. Augustine he declares:

"For it is what we do daily when we partake of his flesh, as before receiving we adore it, not only without superstition, but with all the merit of faith. . . ."[22]

Though Bolton mentions an "interior adoration," by which he was most likely referring to internal prayers and declarations of praise and glorification, he also mentions in his sermon quite openly a form of adoration that was not at all interior, namely, the Corpus Christi procession.

He states in his discourse: "It might be asked what foundation is there for that ceremony usually practised this day in Catholic countries, in carrying our Saviour's body in procession and pomp."[23] Bolton answers that on this day the church recommends the body of the saviour be carried by the hands of the priest in ". . . . memory of his having carried himself, when he distributed his own flesh and blood to his apostles."[24] The explanations given by Augustine and Francis de Sales are also offered, namely that the procession is in commemoration of Christ's having visited the towns and villages of Palestine, and in reparation for his passion in the streets of Jerusalem, respectively.[25] Such a procession is a fitting honor for the Eucharist for,

. . . we may conclude then that there is no degree of glory and worship which is not strictly do to the flesh of Jesus Christ, and that Jesus Christ himself after so noble an alliance cannot due too much to honour his flesh.[26]

The question can rightly be asked whether any such processions in fact took place within the thirteen colonies (later states) of Anglo-America, given the fact that Bolton specifically refers to "Catholic countries" in the quotation cited above. Certainly there is no evidence that such processions were conducted in the midst of the thoroughfares of any of the larger cities of the Eastern seaboard. Still, mention is made of such a procession taking place at the Jesuit mission church at Goshenhoppen, Pennsylvania (the present-day community of Bally), during the course of which it was mistaken by Protestant spectators for a military drill. This incident moved the Pennsylvania Assembly in 1757 to pass a law preventing Catholics from bearing arms.[27] The existence of this procession, combined with another which took place in Baltimore on the occasion of the dedication of the chapel of Saint Mary's seminary on Corpus Christi, 1808,[28] and Bolton's presumption that his audience had some familiarity with such an event, suggests that the devotional practice of the Corpus Christi procession was not unknown in colonial Anglo-America, though its extent and frequency are certainly far from adequately established.

It logically follows from the emphasis placed by these preachers upon the majestic aspect of Christ in the Eucharist, such that Christians should tremble in his presence and prostrate themselves in adoration before him, that a high degree of purity would be required of anyone who would wish to receive Communion. Pile notes in his discussion on the various titles of the Eucharist that "We stile it the bread of angels, because to draw nourishment to our souls from it, we must approach it with the purity of Angels."[29] Frambach declares:

What greater incivility, what greater crime can a man be guilty of, than to entertain so great a guest as God himself, amidst a rabble of worldly and sinful affections, and an unruly multitude of carnal appetites, and revengefull passions. God almighty will execute justice and judgement on them, that defile and profane his sanctuary, by receiving the holy of holies with a soul polluted with willful sin, or sinful inclinations.[30]

Not only should those conscious of actual sin refrain from receiving the Sacrament, but even those who harbor "sinful inclinations" should be wary of communicating. If a listener were to ask, at this point in Frambach's sermon, the degree of purity necessary to receive the Eucharist, he would have had this question answered within minutes, as the homilist subsequently notes that:

> We ought to be as pure and spotless to receive God in the Sacrament as to see him in heaven. Nay, if we consider the actions of our Saviour, we shall find that he seems to require a greater and more diligent preparation from us, when we are to receive him in the Sacrament, than [when] we are to see him in glory.[31]

His reasons for making this rather startling statement are drawn from the New Testament, as he comments that, while Christ washed the feet of his disciples before they ate the Last Supper, he required no such purification prior to his transfiguration on Mount Tabor.[32] Thus he would appear to be arguing that a greater purity is needed to meet Christ in the Eucharist than in the beatific vision undoubtedly moving his listeners to a quite searching examination of conscience—which was his intent.

Should anyone, despite the quite ominous warnings of his preacher, dare to receive the Sacrament either without adequate preparation or in a state of sinfulness, then he would be labeled "an unworthy communicant" and compared to the traitorous apostle Judas. Sewall states "Let not a Judas present himself . . . that is no traitor, no hypocrite, no revenger of injuries, no unjust dealer, no detractor, no lustful soul, no libertine. . . ."[33] Frambach is even more direct when he comments:

> We have a terrible example of an unworthy communicant in that treacherous disciple Judas. Scarce had this unworthy communicant, being polluted with an avaritious affection to money, received this divine morsel, but behold, he is punished by being given up unto Satan.[34]

Sewall concurs in this judgement when he notes that, for an unworthy communicant, the Eucharist ". . . becomes a Sacrament of death and an eternal death."[35] Thus considering the absolute majesty of God, the manifest sinfulness of man, and mindful of the warning of Paul in I Cor 11:27ff. ("and so anyone who eats the bread and drinks the cup of the Lord unworthily . . ."), the faithful are warned in the most dire of terms (e.g. the comparison with Judas) that, should they be conscious of any sins or sinful desires within themselves, it would be better not to receive the Eucharist in this state.

Were the preachers to leave their flock with such thoughts, and make no endeavor to offer a remedy to their predicament, then it would certainly be fair to say that the catechesis of that day and age was not tailored to foster and promote the frequent reception of the Eucharist. This was certainly true of the spirituality associated with the Jansenist movement, which stressed that perfect contrition for one's sins was necessary before the reception of the Eucharist. However, almost every sermon examined in this study stresses the manifest importance of frequent Communion, which was itself a characteristic of the Jesuit's response to the rigorist Jansenist spirituality. Yet how is this advocacy of frequent Communion reconciled with the above position which emphasized man's unworthiness? The answer, at least in part, is provided by the Sacrament of Penance. Sewall makes this clear when he proclaims that the ". . . the scandalous and the impious . . . are excluded [from the Eucharist] as long as they remain in their sins, they are excluded whilst they refuse to purify their hearts by the Sacrament of Penance."[36] Frambach declares, "If you are not pure and innocent, wash off all sins with the cleansing water of penitential tears, and make yourselves fit to receive the true body and blood in the most Blessed Sacrament."[37] Because of the availability of forgiveness and cleansing through the Sacrament of Penance, there is no reason for anyone to fail to receive Communion, save, as Roels notes, that we ". . . wont keep clos to the service of God and bid farewell to our beastly impurities, scandals, detractions, and injustices; because we like to wallow in the mire of sin and follow our scandalous licentiousnesses."[38] Yet the only antidote to the hold of sin on the lives of Christians is the frequent reception of the Eucharist. "It is vain for anyone to plead against frequent Communion," says Frambach,

> It is in vain to say, they are unworthy, because it is in every one's power to remedy that. It is in every one's power to clear his conscience by a good and sincere confession. . . . . . of those that approach to Divine Communion but once a year, not one in a thousand lives long in the state of grace. . . . If you, Dear Christians . . . would take up a custom of communicating oftener, very likely you would be more worthy every day; whereas the longer you abstain through sloth from this Divine Banquet, the worse you grow.[39]

Therefore, if these sermons stress the manifestness of man's sinfulness, it is only in order to encourage the faithful, after cleansing themselves of their misdeeds, to adopt a habit of more frequent Communion, by which their sinful habits will be corrected and their love of God increased.

Truly, some of the strongest language used by the preachers is directed against those who present themselves for Communion only once a year, and then with inadequate preparation. Sewall criticizes those

> . . . who pass over whole years without making one serious reflection on their salvation, who lead their days in every kind of libertinism, and never communicate but when the precept obliges them. . . ."[40]

It is not enough, the argument runs, for Catholics to come once a year to Communion, and then only to fulfill their Easter duty.[41] ". . . How many are there," Roels exclaims, "who slight Jesus, by receiving him only once a year, when they ought to receive him daily. . . ."[42] In another sermon Roels asks,

But alas! What effect can be hop'd from its [the Eucharist] vertue, if by a natural disteast, shameful tepidity, by a culpable negligence, by a pretended humility you receive it not? By consequence if you are desirous to profit by it you must often receive it. . . .[43]

Sewall declares that those of a tepid piety ". . . are contented once at most in the course of the whole year to receive this heavenly food, which our Redeemer has established for our dayly bread."[44] Bolton, when quoting St. Augustine on the adoration due to the Eucharist, speaks of ". . . what . . . we do daily when we partake of his flesh. . . ." (see note 22 above), and Frambach declares that Christ gives us "daily" his body and blood (see note 11 above).

It must be noted, however, when speaking about "daily" Communion, that it would have been highly unusual for anyone—other than a priest—to have received the Eucharist on a daily basis in the second-half of the eighteenth century; indeed it would have been strongly discouraged. This was due not only to the practical reason that few of the Anglo-American colonists would have had access to daily Mass, but also to the piety of the times. Mother Elizabeth Seton, the first American-born saint and the founder of the Sisters of Charity of St. Joseph, had a fervent devotion to the Eucharist, and yet even she received Communion only three times a week. Her Sulpician superior, William DuBourg, thought it wise to caution her that

> I have often reflected on the danger of frequent regular communions in a community. Repeat very often to our daughters [the sisters of the community] that the Rule does not prescribe any number of communions in the week, but only restricts them to three, leaving it to the prudence of the Directors to permit whom he thinks fit to approach so frequently or render communions more rare with certain individuals.[45]

These strictures, moreover, were placed on a community of religious women, leaving one to wonder what attitude would have prevailed towards a member of the laity who wished to communicate three times a week. Thus when the preachers quoted above urge their listeners to "daily" Communion, the reader must view this phrase not in a literal manner, but rather as a device they used to urge (perhaps shock?) the laity into reconsidering the frequency with which they received the Eucharist. Nevertheless, differing perceptions of "frequent" must not be allowed to obscure the fact that the regular reception of Communion, far from being discouraged by these homilists, was rather encouraged by them as a powerful means through which sinfulness and disaffection from God could be overcome. Though determined to stress the wickedness of receiving Communion without proper preparation, they were equally distressed by what they saw as the reluctance of their flocks to approach the Sacrament at all.

Aware that their exhortations to frequent Communion must be accompanied by a description of the efficacy of the Eucharist, the priests sought to give in their catechesis an explanation of the benefits of the Sacrament, which were seen to be two-fold: namely, that it is both a source of strength in one's earthly life, and a pledge of the eternal life to come.

On the first point, that of the Eucharist as source of

strength in this life, Frambach offers a rather complete description:

> . . . this Divine Sacrament supports our spiritual life by the abundance of graces which it furnishes for the food and nourishment of our souls. [This is the bread] that gives us force against all temptations, that weakens our passions and concupiscences, that enables us to grow daily in virtue. . . .[46]

Diderich likewise asserts that the Blessed Sacrament is a ". . . powerful remedy, to secure us against sin, to dispose our hearts and minds to what is holy and virtuous . . . to hinder our running into a wicked course, a reprobate state. . . ."[47] Roels continues this theme when he says that the Eucharist

> . . . will extinguish and calm in your hearts the fire of concupiscence, it will pacify your thoughts . . . it will regulate your inordinate desires, it will repress the rebellion of your senses and subject them to the Law of God and reason.[48]

In all of these explanations the central element stressed again and again is that the Eucharist is a defense against sin, especially that which these preachers style "concupiscence," or the proclivity of the weakened will to stray after the things of this world, and away from God. Left to its own designs, post-lapsarian human nature tends toward a "wicked course" (Diderich), and can hardly resist the "rebellion of the senses" (Roels), but the grace given in the Eucharist is such that it aids man in turning away from this evil path, and "enables him to grow daily in virtue" (Frambach). So powerful is the grace of Christ which is given to the one receiving it, that Sewall argues that ". . . one

Communion well made is capable of curing all . . . [one's] disorders and weaknesses."[49]

The second benefit of the Eucharist is that it acts as a guarantee of eternal life. Father Diderich, echoing the famous Corpus Christi antiphon *"O sacrum convivium,"* states that "Thus with just reason the Sacrament of Eucharist is called a pledge of future glory and of eternal happiness; it being of itself one of the most powerful motives we have of a sweet secure repose. . . ."[50] Frambach declares that

> This Divine Sacrament, I say, will give a life that is everlasting, according to the expressive words and promises of Christ, saying in St. John sixth chapter "He that eateth my flesh and drinketh my blood hath life everlasting . . . ."[51]

This gift of eternal life, however, is not seen as separate from the first aspect of the Eucharist that was discussed above. The two work in tandem, in the sense that through the very deliverance from temptation and vanquishing of concupiscence, the Christian is already being prepared for eternal life. Though both are presented here separately; nevertheless, in the context of the sermons they are seen as working as a whole, inasmuch as if one lives on this earth in the grace of Christ, he is being readied for an eternal life to be spent in communion with him. Likewise, this pledge of eternal life can not be considered as operating apart from man's daily existence. As Frambach notes immediately following the passage cited above, the Blessed Sacrament ". . . gives us new strength and vigour to carry us on happily in our journey towards heaven."[52]

These above-mentioned reflections on the frequent reception of the Eucharist, and on the benefits that one gains from it, have served to illustrate what was spoken of earlier as the "approachable" aspect of the Sacrament, as opposed to what has been seen as its "awesome" quality. Yet just in the same way that the preachers were not at all reluctant to openly proclaim the gulf that separated the "Divine Sacrament" from the lowly Christian, neither were they loath to profess the approachability of Jesus in the Eucharist. In almost every sermon there is an expression of the love and tenderness that Christ feels for his people, indeed, it was for this reason that he first established the Sacrament. Diderich expresses this quite beautifully when he declares that Christ

. . . will be your comfort in all your troubles, who desires nothing more than to crown and make you ever happy both here and hereafter, as he manifestly shews by the institution of the Eucharist, which as it is a most certain mark of love. . . .[53]

This citation brings together the two benefits of the Eucharist discussed above—that of its giving grace both for "here" and the "hereafter"—and states that the impetus for both of them is the love of God. Frambach tells his listeners that ". . . this Divine Sacrament tends in a particular manner to unite us in a union of love with our God, and to transform us in Christ himself."[54] What degree of closeness could be lacking, if the creator of the world seeks to bind himself to the one receiving him in Communion in a "union of love!" How much more startling is this when one considers that it is contained in the same sermons that proclaim so forthrightly the awesome majesty of God? Yet if God is terrible and forbidding, he is also gentle and welcoming: Roels at one place praises the ". . . splendid banquet Jesus has prepared for us in the excess of his fatherly love, by which he desires to unite us to himself."[55] Elsewhere he tells his audience that Christ desired to

. . . unite and incorporate you with himself; his love
for you was not sufficiently express'd in coming down
from heaven, taking upon him our mortal flesh, but
would extend his love farther, by giving you himself in
the Holy Eucharist. . . .[56]

Some of the preachers express the great love of Jesus for
his people in a different way—for them Jesus is not only
loving Saviour but also friend. Pile says that Christ

. . . still remains with us in a more familiar manner on
our altars, where he invites us not only to converse
with him as a friend, but to receive him into our
breasts. . . ."[57]

When Sewall is describing to his audience who may or may
not approach to receive Communion, he tells each Christian to ask himself ". . . whether he is one of those who
belongs to Jesus Christ, and whom he acknowledges for his
worthy friends. . . ."[58] Here Sewall uses the term "friend
of Christ" to mean roughly the same as "one who is in the
state of grace." One may see, then, in contradistinction to
the afore-mentioned gulf between God and man, an amaz-
ing and touching closeness, so much so that Jesus can be
spoken of as uniting himself to Christians through love, and
as remaining among them as friends. Diderich encapsulates
this feeling by drawing upon a traditional, if somewhat
sentimental, image when he declares to his people that
Christ is waiting

. . . for us upon our altars with open arms, ready to
receive us to hear our petitions, to succour us in our
wants, to redress our miseries, to comfort us in affliction, to strengthen us in temptation, to raise and animate us in dejection, and finally to relieve us in all our
necessities. . . .[59]

It is no coincidence that Father Diderich, one of the priests who most stresses the closeness of God to man, is also the one who is most preoccupied with the calumnies that Christ exposes himself to by making himself so readily available to mankind. Emphasis is placed upon the immanence of Christ's presence in the Eucharist, and Diderich, having emphasized that Christ has ". . . left in our hands his own sacred person unguarded and undefended . . . ," goes on to exclaim how Christ has let himself ". . . be exposed to be insulted and abused purely for the love and benefit of his creatures."[60]

> . . . How many hereticks vomit blasphemies against him? How many libertines make a jest of his real presence! How many impious men profane his sacred body by trampling it underfoot?[61]

Yet these attacks on his sacred person are offered by those who are actively are hostile to him, and thus are in some sense to be expected—no matter how odious they may be. How much more callous and insulting, though, are the insults offered to the Eucharist by church-going Catholics, whose behavior is abominable?

> Good God! How many immodesties and irreverences! Some enter hastily, and go out with precipitation; others cast their eyes everywhere except upon the altar, where Jesus Christ resides. What postures do the greatest part keep? Far from honouring him do they not insult him, by their laughing and talking, by their unchristian behavior? How many criminal looks and desires? How many! O that my head were full of water, and my eyes had a fountain of tears, that I might day and night weep for the injuries offered to Jesus Christ in the Blessed Sacrament.[62]

Believing Catholics are much the more to blame for this behavior, since they know the goodness and the mercy of Christ, and cannot offer ignorance as an excuse. Bolton speaks of such behavior in regard to the adoration given to Christ in the Corpus Christi procession, where he states that such exaltation can only be deemed fitting in light of all the abuses Christ has suffered:

> It [adoration] is for all the scandals we have given him, for all the unworthy Communions of so many hypocritical sinners, for all the Masses celebrated by bad priests, for all our tepidity and coolness in approaching the holy table.[63]

Hence it is not only outright actions of contempt by which the Eucharist is profaned, but even by "unworthy Communions" of the faithful and the masses of "bad priests." Since all have been given such an overwhelming privilege in being able to receive the body and blood of their Saviour, all must take care that they both esteem this Sacrament, and more importantly, avail themselves of it.

Since a number of themes found in these sermons delivered on the feast of Corpus Christi have now been examined, it would be convenient to summarize the salient points. First, as was noted at the outset, all these sermons display a profound sense of faith in the real presence of Christ in the Eucharist. While a number of the preachers make an effort to show the grounds on which this faith is based, none gives the reader any hint that the doctrine was being vocally questioned by the Catholic community at large, though the few references containing terms like "our adversaries" and "hereticks" (notes 14 and 9 respectively) show that the preachers were not insensitive to critiques that had been, and were being leveled against Catholic positions, critiques to which their flocks were no doubt exposed.

Many of these sermons—Bolton's in particular—do stress the reverence that ought to be paid to Christ in the Eucharist, a reverence that includes not only internal but also external adoration, and give as a reason for this the many injustices which Christ endures by his desire to be present among his people. While some of these outrages are committed by unbelievers, the priests have no reluctance in leveling charges of indifference and disrespect against Catholics themselves, leading one to reflect that these Christians were not flawless in the frequency and quality of their worship. This aspect should not be overstated, though, as it is known from sermons of an even more venerable age that pastors from the earliest centuries of Christianity were wont to upbraid their people in this regard. Nonetheless, from the remarks that have been quoted on the Easter Duty it would seem that frequent Communion was not common, and that deportment in church left room for improvement.[64]

If there is one theme that is reiterated again and again in these sermons, it is the benefits of, and the necessity for, frequent Communion. The priests deplore the laxity of religious life that they observe, and declare that its surest remedy lies in a more frequent and, it must be added, more devoted reception of the Eucharist. Though they insist on the requisite purity that is deemed necessary to approach the Sacrament—and to expect them to do otherwise is unrealistic given the theological tenor of the times, even if in some cases (e.g. Frambach's) the degree of purity required may seem excessive—they are quick to declare that the Sacrament of Penance exists precisely to provide all with a means to achieve this purity (and here Frambach, for all his rigor, is the one who declares "it is in everyone's power to clear his conscience by a good and sincere confession." See note 39), and therefore approach the altar in a proper state of preparedness. They delineate quite beautifully the various ways that the Eucharist acts in the communicants' life, and a number state openly that Christ unites the communicant to himself in a bond of love and friendship.

These reflections should demonstrate the important place that the Eucharist held in the life of the colonial Anglo-American Catholic community of the eighteenth century. It was believed to play a central role in the life of the Catholic Christian, guarding and strengthening him against the snares and temptations of this world, and preparing him to share in the glories of the hereafter.

Notes

1. Quotations from the sermons have been altered in the following ways: abbreviations have been replaced, capitalization and punctuation have been modernized, but spelling has been left in its original form.

2. For information on the celebration of Corpus Christi in French and Spanish colonial America, see Z. Englehardt, *The Missions and Missionaries of California,* (San Francisco), I (1908), 48ff., III (1910), 27; R.G. Thwaites, *Jesuit Relations and Allied Documents,* (Cleveland, 1896–1901), Vol. 30, 181, Vol. 32, 89 ff., noted in Francis X. Weiser, *Handbook of Christian Feasts and Customs* (New York: Harcourt, Brace and Co., 1952), 267.

3. American Catholic Sermon Collection, Special Collections, Lauinger Library, Georgetown University, Washington, D.C. (hereafter ACSC), Pi-26 (fragment).

4. ACSC, Se-15, Di-14, Bol-21.

5. ACSC, Fr-1, Ro-8.

6. ACSC, Se-15.

7. ACSC, Pi-26.

8. *Ibid.*

9. ACSC, Se-15.

10. ACSC, Fr-1.

11. *Ibid.*

12. ACSC, Ro-8.

13. ACSC, Bol-21.

14. ACSC, Di-14.

15. *Ibid.*

16. *Ibid.*

17. ACSC, Fr-1.

18. *Ibid.*

19. John 1:1 ff.

20. ACSC, Di-14.

21. ACSC, Bol-21.

22. *Ibid.*

23. *Ibid.*

24. *Ibid.*

25. *Ibid.*

26. *Ibid.*

27. Gerald Fogarty, "The Origins of the Mission, 1634–1773," in *The Maryland Jesuits, 1634–1833*, R. Emmet Curran, et.al. (Baltimore: The Corporation of Roman Catholic Clergymen, 1976), 24.

28. Annabelle M. Melvile, *Louis William DuBourg: Bishop of Louisiana and the Floridas, Bishop of Montauban, and the Archbishop of Besancon, 1766–1833*, 2 Vols. (Chicago: Loyola University Press, 1986), Vol. I, p. 145.

29. ACSC, Pi-26.

30. ACSC, Fr-1.

31. *Ibid.*

32. *Ibid.*

33. ACSC, Se-15.

34. ACSC, Fr-1.

35. ACSC, Se-15.

36. *Ibid.*

37. ACSC, Fr-1.

38. ACSC, Ro-4.

39. ACSC, Fr-1.

40. ACSC, Se-15.

41. This precept, which obliged the laity to annually confess their serious sins and receive the Eucharist—fulfilling the duty during the Easter season, hence the name "Easter duty"—had been binding on Catholics since the time of the Fourth Lateran Council in 1215. H. Denzinger and A. Schönmetzer, *Enchiridion Symbolorum, Definitionem et Declarationem de rebus fidei et morum* (Herder: Freiburg im Breisgau, 1965), no. 812.

42. ACSC, Ro-8.

43. ACSC, Ro-4.

44. ACSC, Se-15.

45. Quoted in Ellin Kelly and Annabelle Melville, *Elizabeth Seton: Selected Writings* (New York: Paulist Press, 1987), 69.

46. ACSC, Fr-1.

47. ACSC, Di-14.

48. ACSC, Ro-4.

49. ACSC, Se-15.

50. ACSC, Di-14. The Antiphon is found in the Second Vespers of the Office of Corpus Christi: "O sacrum convivium, in quo

Christus sumitur; recolitur memoria passionis eius; mens imple-
tur gratia; et futurae gloriae nobis pignus datur, alleluia." ["O
holy Banquet, in which Christ is received, in which the memory
of His Passion is renewed, in which the soul is filled with grace
and a pledge of future glory is given us, alleluia!"]. For the
complete Office see: *The Hours of the Divine Office in English
and Latin,* ed. Leonard J. Doyle, et al., vol. II., (Collegeville,
MN: Liturgical Press, 1963), pp. 1470ff.

51. ACSC, Fr-1.
52. *Ibid.*
53. ACSC, Di-14.
54. ACSC, Fr-1.
55. ACSC, Ro-8.
56. *Ibid.*
57. ACSC, Pi-26.
58. ACSC, Se-15.
59. ACSC, Di-14.
60. *Ibid.*
61. *Ibid.*
62. *Ibid.*
63. ACSC, Bol-21.
64. Comments on the morality and sacramental practice of
Catholics in late eighteenth century colonial Anglo-America may
be found in the report of 1 March, 1785 that John Carroll, recently
appointed to the post of Superior of the American Catholic
missions in 1784, sent to Cardinal Antonelli of Propaganda Fidei.
For a translation see John Gilmary Shea, *History of the Catholic
Church in the United States,* II, (New York: John G. Shea, 1888),
257–261.

Dearest Christians: A Study of Eighteenth Century Anglo-American Catholic Ecclesiology

Raymond J. Kupke

Avery Dulles, in his seminal work on ecclesiology, *Models of the Church,* examines the life and mission of the Catholic Church by focusing on five different facets of the nature of the Church, or, if you will, five different "ways of being church," namely, Church as institution, sacrament, community, herald, and servant.[1] For Dulles, an American Jesuit priest of the Maryland Province, these models of the Church were partially the result not only of a lifetime of study and reflection, but also of a life lived within the Church, as experienced through the broad spectrum of liturgy, education, social action, and community life which are the ordinary experience of the American Catholic. Indeed, these aspects of church life are so visible that they give even the non-Catholic and the anti-Catholic some basis from which to formulate an image of the Church.

Two centuries before Avery Dulles there were other Jesuit priests, serving on the "Maryland Mission," the forerunner of the present Maryland Province, who strove in vastly different circumstances to convey to a small, insular, and threatened flock their own model of ecclesiology, an adequate sense of what it means to be Catholic. This study will seek to explore the sense of the Church conveyed to eighteenth century Anglo-American Catholics as revealed through the surviving sermons of the Maryland Jesuits preserved in the Special Collections of the Lauinger Memorial Library at Georgetown University.[2]

The presence of the Jesuits in Maryland dated from the very beginning of the colony. At the invitation of the proprietor, Cecil Calvert, two Jesuit priests, Andrew White and John Altham, and a brother, Thomas Gervase, were part of the initial contingent of settlers who sailed from England on *The Ark* and *The Dove* in November 1633.[3] Calvert, a Catholic himself, had assured freedom of religion in the new colony and had thus attracted a number of his co-religionists. As with all missionaries to the New World, the Maryland Jesuits were keenly interested in the conversion of the native Indians, as well as the spiritual welfare of the colonists. While some successful initiatives were made among the Piscataways and the Patuxents, the overthrow of the Calverts in 1645 brought an end to the Indian missions and the expulsion of the Jesuits themselves. When the Jesuits were able to return to Maryland in 1648 they found their circumstances vastly changed. The Protestant ascendancy in the colony, as well as the strained circumstances of the Indians themselves, meant an end to any real missionary efforts among the natives. Instead the Maryland Jesuits were reduced to a low-profile ministry among the Maryland Catholics, and satisfied their missionary instincts by slowly widening the arc of their endeavors to include the few scattered Catholics of Delaware, New Jersey, New York, Pennsylvania, and Virginia.

One hundred and fifty-six Jesuits served on the Maryland Mission from 1633 until the dissolution of the society in 1773, of whom some thirty were brothers. They were never very numerous at any one time, numbering twenty-three in 1773. All were educated, professed and ordained in Europe.

I studied the sermons of eighteen of these men, as well as those of one non-Jesuit, Germain Barnabas Bitouzey, who entered the United States in 1794. Of these nineteen, seven (John and Sylvester Boarman, John Boone, John Carroll, Henry and Leonard Neale, and Charles Sewall) were native Marylanders; six (George Hunter, Augustine Jenkins, Robert Molyneux, Joseph Mosley, Henry Pile, and John Williams) were English; Bitouzey and Benjamin Louis Roels were Belgians, Ferdinand Farmer and Matthias Manners were Germans, James Carroll was Irish, and John Baptist Diderich was a Luxemburger.[4] Henry Neale was the oldest of the group, having been born in Maryland in 1702. Leonard Neale, born in 1747, was the youngest. One of the group surveyed, George Hunter, would serve as superior of the Maryland Mission in 1756–1763. John Carroll became the first American Catholic bishop (of Baltimore in 1789) and archbishop (in 1808), and was succeeded by another of those surveyed, Leonard Neale.

To support themselves the Jesuits imitated their neighbors and engaged in farming, eventually acquiring nearly 13,000 acres in seven plantations (Bohemia, Deer Creek, Newtown, Port Tobacco, St. Inigoes, White Marsh, and Tuckahoe) which served as places of worship in the absence of parish churches. The names of these plantations, as well as those of smaller Mass stations such as Elk River, Potomac, Sakia, and Wye, turn up regularly at the head of the surveyed sermons. Most of the Jesuits lived at these plantations dividing their time between plantation management and a circuit-riding ministry. Joseph Mosley founded the plantation at Tuckahoe in Talbot County in 1765 and led a very isolated existence on Maryland's Eastern Shore until his death in 1787. Robert Molyneux and Ferdinand Farmer, on the other hand, led a more cosmopolitan existence caring for St. Joseph's in Philadelphia. Indeed at the time of his death in 1786 Farmer was both a member of the

Philosophical Society of Philadelphia and a trustee of the University of Pennsylvania.[5]

The congregations served by the Jesuits of the Maryland Mission consisted of communities clustered around their own plantations which were served on a weekly basis, and Mass stations at various homes at some distance from the plantation which were visited on a monthly basis. The Sunday routine consisted of confessions, followed by Mass, with a sermon preached after Mass explaining Catholic doctrine. In this manner, for example, Joseph Mosley served a congregation of from 500 to 600 communicants on Maryland's Eastern Shore.[6] Nevertheless, the Catholics of Maryland, numbering some three thousand in the 1708 census, never amounted to more than one-eighth of the colony's total population. At the end of the eighteenth century John Carroll estimated that Maryland had twenty thousand Catholics who comprised two-thirds of the Catholic population of the new nation.

Although Maryland's eighteenth-century Catholics were theoretically under the same penal laws as their co-religionists in England, in practice these laws were not applied systematically or harshly. Nonetheless, Maryland Catholics were unable to vote or hold public office. They were barred from certain professions. They could not worship publicly, nor establish Catholic schools.[7]

Despite the political and religious disadvantages, several of Maryland's Catholic families, including the Brookes, Carrolls, Digges, and Taneys, did amass considerable fortunes and were able to extend a certain degree of aid and respectability to their fellow Catholics. They were also able, despite existing laws to the contrary, to send their children abroad for a Catholic education on the Continent. This exposure, not only to a Catholic education, but also to the fullness of Catholic life and culture, led to a number of both male and female religious vocations in the eighteenth century. The Society of Jesus itself received thirty-six novices from Maryland during a century and a quarter.

The number of religious vocations among these Marylanders educated abroad points to the religious poverty of native Maryland Catholic life. For Maryland's Catholics, religious life was always a shadow existence. Many of the features which were the hallmark of the fullness of a Catholic atmosphere elsewhere were denied them. They were unable to build suitable churches, as were their neighbors, nor to conduct worship fully and publicly. Despite the brief existence of two schools, they were unable to provide a Catholic education for their children except in a most rudimentary manner at home. With the exception of those Catholics who had been to the Continent, Maryland's Catholics had never seen a bishop, or a religious sister, or a charitable institution under Catholic auspices. Indeed, in 1773 Ferdinand Farmer responded negatively through the Bishop of Quebec to Rome's inquiry about the suitability of a bishop for America. Part of his fear was that a religious person "established in dignity" would arouse the hatred of non-Catholics, who also had no bishop in America.[8]

So far removed from ordinary Catholic jurisdiction were they that when the Jesuits were disbanded in 1773 and ordered to affiliate with the local Church jurisdiction, the Maryland Jesuits had no local diocese to affiliate with, and had to incorporate themselves as a civic entity and agree to their own set of rules to maintain their own discipline and order and to preserve their plantations until John Carroll was given some limited jurisdiction from Rome in 1784.[9]

Not only were Maryland Catholics deprived of many devotional aspects of their religion, but even the essential sacramental system was experienced only in an abbreviated way. The first ordination in English-speaking America did not take place until 1793. Generations of Maryland Catholics never completed the Sacraments of Christian Initiation because Confirmation was not celebrated in the colonies until the faculty to confirm was granted to John Carroll in 1784. Given the scattered nature of Maryland's Catholics and the few priests, many Catholics died without the Last Rites of the Church.

It is in this atmosphere that the eighteen surveyed priests of the Maryland Mission preached, and through their preaching sought to convey a sense of Church.

THE REIGN OF GOD IS LIKE . . .

The preaching style of the eighteenth century Maryland Jesuits differs in several respects from that of the twentieth century. Trained in Belgium and France, the Maryland Jesuits were deeply influenced by the spirituality of the old French masters, especially Francis de Sales and Jacques Benigne Bossuet. This piety,

> . . . was rooted in an anthropology that was moderately positive about human nature and promoted a spirituality that stressed virtuous living as a key to happiness.[10]

Although the sermons often centered on concrete examples taken from the Biblical texts of the annual lectionary then in use, the Jesuits just as often felt free to diverge from the given texts and focus on catechetical themes, such as the creed, the sacraments, the marks of the Church, or on topics associated with living the Christian life, such as profanity and deportment at Mass. Indeed, it sometimes appears that liturgical preaching, as we understand it today, was not the norm in the eighteenth century. As a principal means of Catholic education, it appears that the sermons had a life of their own apart from the liturgical setting, and were sometimes delivered as a catechetical discourse after Mass had been celebrated.

This extra-liturgical character of the sermons would help

to account for the appearance of nearly identical texts in sermons from different preachers as, apparently, good sermons were traded and material borrowed without hesitation. This might also account for the careful way in which the sermons were written down, with corrections and additions, and with Scriptural citations in place. This catechetical use may also account for their length, although, in any case, sermons of this period tended to be of considerable duration and are described by several preachers as "entertainments." Nevertheless, Henry Neale's entertainment "On Faith" for the Third Sunday after Epiphany runs to forty-six notebook pages.[11]

But, if these sermons were not always firmly grounded in the liturgy, they were firmly rooted in Sacred Scripture. The Jesuit preachers made ample use of biblical references both to illustrate their points and to give them a strong backing. Among the points which the preachers derived from their use of Scripture was the identity of the Roman Catholic Church as the true Church established by Christ. John L. McKenzie, commenting on the Gospel parables of the kingdom of God, states: "The kingdom which contains both good and bad is most easily understood as the Church."[12] The Maryland preachers made ample use of this image to help their flock realize that their attachment to the Catholic Church was rooted in Scripture itself. In a lengthy sermon in February 1792 excommunicating John Cause, one of the refractory parishioners of Holy Trinity German Church in Philadelphia, John Carroll, beginning with the text from John 18:36, foreshadowed McKenzie's later exegesis.

The kingdom of God here spoken of is his Church. He did not establish it for worldly purposes, or on worldly principles. The advantages to be obtained in this Church are not, as in the Kingdoms of the world, temporal prosperity and personal security.[13]

Preaching at Newtown on the Sixth Sunday after Epiphany, 1765, on the parable of the Mustard Seed (Matthew 13:31) John Boone begins by stating that "No comparison could give us a more lively, or better description of the beginning, and progress of the Church."[14] Boone speaks on the establishment of the Church as his first point, and as his second,

> . . . the indispensable obligation you live under as members of the Catholic Church, to live according to the pure, and holy maxims of it.[15]

This sermon was also used, almost verbatim, by John Boarman. Still later, in the same sermon, Boone also used the scriptural image of the Church as founded by Christ on the rock of Peter's faith (Matthew 16:13).

> It must be astonishing, and surprising, that any one, who professes to believe the Gospell of Christ, that he is the Son of God, God himself, essentially and invariably true, either to deny these promises, or suppose them not to be made good. Yet, this is the case of many, who boldly charge the whole Christian world with errors. Errors of the worst kind, which destroy the very being of the Church. Christ promised to build his Church upon a rock, and that the gates of Hell should not prevail against her. He has done it! and on this rock she remains, and shall continue, fixed immovably to the end of the world, to the consummation of all things.[16]

In a similar fashion, Leonard Neale used the kingdom parable of a treasure buried in a field (Matthew 13:44) to describe the Church.[17]

But it was not only the kingdom parables which provided the preachers with scriptural allusions to the Church.

Henry Pile, preaching on the Second Sunday after Easter on the text from John 10:16 compared the Church to the sheepfold of Christ.

> Jesus, being the good shepherd, who came to redeem all mankind without exception he therefore tells the Jews, that besides them he has other sheep, which it behooves him to join to them that, as they have but one shepherd, they may make but one fold. These words of the Christ to the Jews inform us in the most natural manner, that our Divine Saviour intended to unite both Jews and Gentiles in the belief and practice of the one religion of which he was the head and founder.[18]

And still another unidentified preacher, holding forth on the January Second Feast of the Holy Name of Jesus, identified the Church with the heavenly Jerusalem of Revelation 21:2.

> In fine, my friends, we are included in the same prophecies with Christ, and have been jointly with him the wish of the nations—the Church was to be the new Jerusalem—the spotless Spouse of Christ—in which God alone is to be acknowledged and adored in spirit and truth.[19]

The word "church" appears only twice in the Gospels themselves, and John Williams used one of these two texts, Matthew 18:17, as the scriptural basis for his short sermon on the Ninth Article of the Creed.

> It is no wonder that our Blessed Saviour, in the words of my text should bid us look upon those, who will not hear the Church as heathens and publicans, since in all her decisions she is guided by that Spirit of Truth,

which he promised would abide with his Disciples for ever (John 14:16, 17) and guides them into all truth (John 16:13). The unerring authority of Christ's Church is so clearly established in these and sundry texts of Holy Scripture, that it seems surprising such as ground all their Faith upon the Written Word of God should waver from it in this fundamental article, and whilst they profess daily in their Creed to believe the Catholic Church refuse submission to its judgement in the most essential points, abandon its faith, and reject its discipline.[20]

A favorite text used by several preachers is Christ's promise to be with the Church until the end of the world (Matthew 28:20). Louis Roels, preaching on the Third Sunday after Epiphany in 1766, is perhaps typical of the preachers who strove to move their congregations to see in this text a scriptural basis for their continued adherence to the Catholic faith and practice in the midst of a hostile world.

Wherefore he has vouchsafed solemnly to engage His infallible word, that he will be with her to the end of the world: that his Holy Spirit shall teach her in all truth, and abide with her, even to the consommation of this world; that the gates of hell shall never prevail against her, and has moreover commanded us to hear and obey the church, as God himself (says) under pain of eternal damnation, he that hears you hears me, and he that despises you despises me as we read in the 16th chapter of St. Luke, as also in the 18th of St. Matthew if he will not hear the Church, let him be to them as a heathen and publican. So that you may see from hence that our belief of the divine mysteries upon Christ's authority is a true Christian saving faith; there certainly is no doubt that, but Christ has this authority, the apostles had this authority, the holy Church of Christ has this authority.[21]

Roels perhaps best sums up the efforts of all these eighteenth-century Jesuit preachers in their attempt to present the Catholic Church, in the midst of many churches using the Bible, as the one Church firmly rooted in the Scriptures.

Notwithstanding, amidst the diversity of Churches, all pretend to be in the right Church or Faith, we know for certain that there is but one that is the right, for St. Paul in the 4th Chapter to the Ephesians, tells us, one Lord, one faith and one baptism; therefore says St. Austin, the Church is either one or none, and this one true church must be the one which Christ ordered to be established; for no other Church has power to teach, nor sufficient authority to be believed.[22]

THE FAITHFUL REMNANT

There have been many times in the history of the Church when a particular local church underwent, for a period of time, persecution and separation from the ordinary communication with the rest of the Catholic world. We have only to recall the example of the Church in France during the Reign of Terror, the Church in Germany during the *Kulturkampf,* and the Church in various Eastern European countries in our own day. However with the exception of the miraculous preservation of the underground Church in Japan from the sixteenth to the nineteenth centuries, few church histories can rival that of the colonial Maryland Church for perseverance.

As we have already seen, the Church in Maryland was not only founded in an atmosphere of oppression, but continued largely isolated from the wider Church, for nearly a century and a half. It was the task of the Maryland Jesuits, utilizing their sermons as the principal means at their disposal, to preserve their flock intact as Catholic believers and at the same time to give their isolated coreligionists a sense of what it means to be Catholic, to be connected to a universal Church.

Germain Bitouzey, preaching on Matthew 7:15 on the Seventh Sunday after Pentecost, hammered home the notion of the one true Church of which the colonial Catholics were a part.

> We see, Christians, in this world, particularly in this country, we see a great variety of worships and religions; and yet there is but one true, there is but one that can lead us to heaven; and this is the one religion Jesus Christ instituted when he was in the world.
>
> Since then there is but one true religion, it is a matter of great consequence to us to know what that religion is, and to know in what church this religion is carefully preserved and taught, that we may live conformably to its principles, and thus work out the salvation of our souls, and that we may be happy in the world to come for ever and ever.[23]

After his appointment as superior of the American missions in 1784, John Carroll sought to acquaint his flock with the Sacrament of Confirmation which he was newly empowered to confer. In stressing to his flock the importance of this sacrament which had hitherto been academic for most Americans, Carroll hit on the same theme.

> The faith of Christ overcame the world. The doctrine of the Gospel enlightened mankind; the darkness and delusions of false religions faded before the resplendant light of Christianity; the Church of God rose

conspicuous on their ruins, and has always remained in the public profession of the same faith, in the teaching of the same doctrines, in the administration of the same Sacraments, in the possession of the same ministry uninterruptedly derived from Christ and his Apostles, in the offering of the same one holy and adorable sacrifice to the Eternal Father, and in retaining its distinguishing and characteristic title of Catholic, tho it has been contested by so many sects, which from the earliest and thro all successive ages, have endeavored to wrest it from her and appropriate it to themselves.[24]

In 1789, after election by his fellow priests, John Carroll was appointed first bishop of Baltimore. This coincided with the election of the first bishops of the Protestant Episcopal Church in the same year. Germain Bitouzey sought to clearly establish the position of the bishop as the teacher of the flock and focal point of the community's unity with the whole Church, and at the same time to clear up any confusion the presence of a variety of bishops may have caused.

But to whom shall we apply to learn what we are to believe?

We must apply, Christians, to those to whom Jesus Christ commanded us to apply, and these are the apostles and bishops of that Church in which they are the legitimate successors of the Apostles. Jesus Christ instructed the bishops and gave them to us or gave them to his Church to be our teachers, and he commanded us to hear them.

But that man sees in the world bishops of two different Churches, the bishops of the Catholic Church, and the bishops of the Protestant Church, and he does not know to whom of these he is to apply that he may learn for certain what he is to believe.

Now it must appear then very certain to that man who cannot read and to those who can read, that it is more safe and more secure to follow the doctrine of the Catholic Church than the doctrine of the Protestant Church.[25]

Germain Bitouzey, in striving to help his flock see clearly the distinction between their Catholic faith and the faith of the other Christian churches by which they were surrounded, reduced the articles which divided the two churches into five: the number of sacraments, auricular confession, the real presence of Christ in the Eucharist, belief in purgatory, and belief in the intercession of the saints. In discussing these points of divergence, Bitouzey proposed to his hearers the ingenious argument that the Catholic Church is preferable, not merely because she is right, but because she incorporates within her belief all that the Protestants believe and more, and thus the believer receives more security for his faith.

This instruction is intended to help that man how to make that examination and he will find that in matters of faith the doctrine of the Catholic Church is best, and that it affords a greater security, and therefore that it deserves the preference over the Protestant Church. Why is it so? Because the Catholic Church believes everything that is believed in the Protestant Church, if therefore the Protestant Church is right in its faith and doctrine, then the Catholic Church is also right because in our Church we believe everything that the Protestant Church believes; and the Protestant Church can not say the same. For if the faith and doctrine of the Catholic Church is right, then the faith and doctrine of the Protestant Church is wrong, because they don't believe everything we do. Therefore if they are right, we are right with them, and if we are right they are wrong. This begins to show a little that the Catholic Church affords a greater security of salvation, and therefore that it deserves the preference over the Protestant Church.[26]

After American Independence, the Catholics in the new nation had the opportunity to profess their faith publicly. While they no doubt appreciated this new freedom, at the same time there must have been some hesitation within the flock in getting used to these new possibilities. John Carroll, in a sermon entitled, "Confess our Religion Exteriorly," tried to impress on his flock the importance not only of holding on to the faith, but of giving public witness to it.

For when it pleased God to institute a religion here on earth he surely did not intend that it remain hidden in darkness and sequestered from the eyes of mankind. As it is to serve to glorify him, it cannot be sufficient for it to remain shut up in the secret of men's hearts: it must be visible and by its splendor contribute to raise in us ideas worthy of the greatness of the master to whom it subjects us and proposes as the object of our worship. For this purpose were ordained the publick ceremonies of religion.[27]

Joseph Mosley, speaking at Sakia on December 4, 1760, touched on the same issue with regard to the use of the Sign of the Cross.

Therefore, let no Catholick, when he is known, ever be ashamed of it in whatever company he finds himself, for to be ashamed of it, is as I may, a tacit denial of your Faith.[28]

Other Jesuits, too, strove to keep their flocks connected to the visible links with the universal Church. Augustine Jenkins reminded his people to pray for the pope and the bishops.

> Thus the priest first offers to God for the pope, head of the Church, and vicar of Jesus Christ who governs it under him. Then for the bishop, who by the institution of Christ governs the respective diocese.[29]

John Boarman, commenting on the extension of the Feast of the Sacred Heart to the universal Church in 1765, describes the decree,

> Rome, dearest Christians, has spoken, the voice of Peter has been heard in that of Clement the XIII and the Solemnity of the Sacred Heart of Jesus is established with an authentical and uniform worship throughout the whole Catholick world.[30]

John Diderich sought to make his flock aware of the Jubilee Year proclaimed by Pope Clement XIV for 1775 (the same pontiff who had dissolved the Society of Jesus two years earlier) and to connect them to the piety of the universal Church.

> Let us then resolve to make good use of the present time, as the only we can make sure of, particularly the holy time of the approaching Jubilee, when all the entrances of heaven are open to every truly pentitent sinner.[31]

In striving to preserve the faith of their people, the Maryland Jesuits seem to be much more sensitive to the dangers arising from religious indifferentism than with concerns about defections to other Christian sects. Like the

Jesuits themselves some of the best minds in the new nation had been schooled in Europe. Men like Thomas Paine, Benjamin Franklin, and Thomas Jefferson were willing to embrace a vague notion of God, but were indifferent to the claims of any organized religion. More so than their flock, Carroll and the other Jesuits had been exposed to these same ideas on the Continent and were quick to warn their people about the dangers resulting from these errors. On taking possession of his new see at Baltimore on December 12, 1790, John Carroll warned against these dangers.

> But there are others (duties) still more burthensome to be borne by me in this particular portion of Christ's Church, which is committed to my charge and where every thing is to be raised as it were from its foundation.
> . . . to preserve their faith untainted amidst the contagion of error, surrounding them on all sides; to preserve in their hearts a warm charity and forebearance towards every other denomination of Christians; and at the same time to preserve them from that fatal and prevailing indifference which views all religions as equally acceptable to God and salutary to men.[32]

Rorbert Molyneux, preaching on Paul's insistence on the Gospel (I Corinthians 5: 1–2) on the Eleventh Sunday after Pentecost, sallied forth to do battle with indifferentism in very practical terms.

> The readiness of too many to hear falsehood and error, is a sign that they do not stick fast to the Ghospel and that they have grounds to fear, that the Ghospel does not save them. The libertinism of opinions never ran higher than in the present ages, and the reason this libertinism does not always produce sects, that separate from the Church, is, because these libertines have

no religion enough at heart to expose themselves to the consequences of a visible schism. But tho' they remain in the communion of the Church, they do not nevertheless remain in its faith.[33]

Charles Sewall, preaching on the sending of the Holy Spirit (Acts 2:5) also spoke strongly against those who tried to remain within the Catholic fold but also embrace the new ideas.

Yes, it is the spirit of the world which now threatens America, not only with irreligion, deism and atheism, but with all the otherisms and temporal miseries and calamities under which almost all Europe now groans and laments. For what is it we behold! Alas, everywhere men judge according to the spirit of the world, they act, they govern themselves according to the spirit of the world; and many even have a mind to serve their God according to the spirit of the world.[34]

John Diderich sums up the efforts of the Maryland Jesuits to convey to their flocks a sense of their Catholic religion and heritage, and a conviction to remain steadfast within it.

Is it possible, after the infinite proofs you have given us of your excess of love towards man, that you could leave him without an infallible guide, whereby to distinguish your wise salutary truths from the abominable inventions of the devil? Christians, away with such sentiments. Remember your crucified Jesus has promised to be with his beloved spouse the Church until the very end of the world.[35]

APOLOGETICS AND POLEMICS

Father George Hunter, speaking to his congregation in 1775, mentions the presence of a newly-baptized adult in the congregation.

The words of my text I hope I may presume may be justly applied to each one of the present assembly, but to no one so properly as to you in particular new-born Christian being newly born to Christ by the sacrament of Baptism, the consequence of your faith and belief in Jesus Christ the Lord and Redeemer of mankind; we therefore justly congratulate you as a distinguished favorite of heaven . . . your embracing our persuasion preferrable to all others after having implored in a due manner unerring Providence to direct you to the right way, ought to be looked on by all present as an additional proof or confirmation of their being in the only true and right way to a happy futurity.[36]

The acknowledgement of this convert points to another feature of eighteenth-century Anglo-American preaching, namely, debate with the Protestant majority sects, and the winning of converts to the faith. Robert Emmett Curran mentions that the absence of organized Protestant churches in the earliest years of the Maryland Colony contributed to a rather high number of converts.[37] However the Puritan ascendancy in the middle of the seventeenth century, the establishment of the Anglican Church in 1702, and the more rigid enforcement of anti-Catholic measures made winning converts a dangerous business. Nevertheless a small number of converts continued throughout the colonial period, and several prominent Maryland families had Catholic branches by the time of Independence. Joseph Mosley, preaching on Paul's acknowledgement of the Thessalonians' difficulties (I Thessalonians 2:6) on the Sixth Sunday after Epiphany in 1758 likened the tribulations of his own flock to those of Paul.

> And it is the same reason, dearest Christians, that induces me to think it my indispensable obligation to encourage you to bear firmly and steadily all calumnies and persecutions, that are raised in our heretical country by our inveterate enemy.
>
> No one can show greater love than by laying down his life for his friends. Now dearest Christians, if Christ has said that no one can show greater love, than by dying for his friend, and since such an occasion of happiness won't in all probability befall any of us in regard of God, I may from these same words bring a lawful consequence, that he that comes the nearest death, will also show the greatest love. I believe there is no one, that has experienced it, will deny injuries, affronts, loss of estates, afflictions, tribulations, incapacity of publick offices, to approach the nearest death, anything can in this life. Nay, even the loss of honors and good name is reputed by some to be worse than death itself. You see then, dearest Christians, it is by tribulations that our love is put to the test, it is tried by them, as gold in the glowing furnace.[38]

Henry Pile also understood the real life difficulties of practicing the faith when he recalled the penances of the Lenten Season.

> . . . this was the reason [you] embraced the penitential practice of fasting and abstinence at appointed times of the year, and this in short the reason why you are contended to be rebuked and reviled by friends and relations, by neighbours and country men; for convinced [of] the truth of the religion and the necessity of practicing it in order to save your souls, you there-

fore put up with every other inconvenience and place your happiness in suffering and contradiction sooner than renounce those principles of belief which you are convinced beyond the probability of a rational doubt, to be the true law of Christ, and the only means of saving your immortal souls.[39]

Joseph Mosley, speaking in 1758 reminded his congregation of the example of the English martyrs who had preceded them.

I'll only propose to you your own countrymen, who, only in the last century chose rather to be hanged under that bloody standard of the holy Martyrs, than suffer themselves to be robbed of the Faith in which they so much gloried. We see them hurried to prison, tortured on a rack, accused by false witnesses, condemned, dragged thro the streets, hanged and quartered. Faith was the cause. Love shoved them on. It was nothing but Divine Love that made them sustain these dreadful torments, and could you, dearest Christians, in proof of the same love, undergo the loss of your estates and permit yourselves to be accounted fools for your Master Jesus Christ.[40]

Several preachers attempted to attest to the truth of the Catholic faith and the error of other churches by means of the four "marks" of the Church which were traditionally seen as proofs of her divine institution.

Christ has revealed his divine mysteries to the Catholick Church, he has bountifully promised and solemnly engaged his divine word, that she shall teach truth, and left marks by which we may know her, to wit, unity, sanctity, Catholicity, and apostolicity, and where these marks are not found, you may depend on your being in the wrong Church.[41]

Henry Pile was more polemical in attributing to the Catholic Church the four marks which are the proof of the true church.

But ask the Church of England or any other reformed Church to prove her right to the four marks of the Church of Christ: surely she is able to produce no weak proof therefore. Before the time of Luther, Calvin, and Henry the 8th in what part of the known world did the reformed churches exist? The plain and fair answer is no where. For all the world can tell when they made their appearance and no single writer ever mentioned one syllable of them before. As to unity of faith they have none, unless the scriptures interpreted by each one's private sense is the rule of faith.[42]

One of the areas of difference between the Catholic Church and the other Christian churches is the sacraments. Not only do Catholics and Protestants differ in their belief on the number of sacraments instituted by Christ, but they also have serious differences in their understanding of the very nature of sacraments themselves. The real presence of Christ in the Eucharist, for example, was a cause of dissension between the churches, and provided several Anglo-American preachers with an opportunity to expound on Catholic doctrine. John Diderich, speaking on the feast of Corpus Christi at Elk River in June 1783, spoke of the reasonableness of the Eucharistic mystery.

The great, august and glorious mystery which the Church solemnizes at this time, namely of the Blessed Eucharist, is one of those articles of our faith which has met with the greatest opposition from all the reformers of religion. Their chief pretended difficulty, is that it is contrary to their senses, which heaven has given them as their directors in life. I call it pretended because it is no more than what they surmount in other cases as well natural as supernatural. How consistent they are to the pretended difficulty in believing the sun to be of a greater size than the earth tho' their senses seem to tell them the contrary.

Likewise for the belief of the Eucharist. The former, or the belief of the sun's being of a greater magnitude than the earth, being at least a thousand times bigger than the whole globe on which we dwell. This, I say, they dare not deny because the testimony of the learned forbids them so to do, which arguments are particularly strong in our case because the universal testimony of the learned part of Christianity, (a very small number within these last two centuries only excepted) agree in this as also their very chief reformer Luther himself, who has expressly left in his writings that he would gladly oppose the doctrine of the Eucharist, but the Scripture was so very clear on that head, that he knew not how to go about to deny it.[43]

Charles Sewall, preaching in 1791, compared the attitude of some Catholics toward the Eucharist to those of the heretics of former days.

It is true that in former days some furious fanatics [hereticks crossed out] carried fire and sword into his temples to destroy them, they have defiled his altars, they have broken down his tabernacles, they have trampled himself underfoot: but after all even in this way they acted in consequence of their error. Whereas by any unsupportable contradiction, faithful and unfaithful at the same time, faithful in belief and speculation, unfaithful in manners and practice, you profane that which you adore.[44]

In addition to the Eucharist, the Sacrament of Penance unknown in the Protestant churches, also provided the preachers with the opportunity to expound on Catholic doctrine in the face of Protestant disbelief. Thus, Augustine Jenkins spoke "On the 10th Article of the Creed—I Believe in the Remission of Sins" at Newton in 1795.

> Thence, we are to believe that in the Church there is remission of sins and that there is a real power given to the pastors of the Church of remitting them by the Sacraments to all that repent. This article is placed in the creed, immediately after the Article of the Church to teach us that it is to the Church alone Jesus Christ has granted the power of forgiving sins, and that we can not receive this grace but in her bosom.[45]

Matthias Manners, speaking at Bohemia Manor on the Thirteenth Sunday after Pentecost in 1764, was more understanding of the Protestant difficulty in understanding this sacrament.

> This is only a power reserved and given to the priests of the new law. To those it is granted to make friends out of the greatest enemies of God, to restore the sanctifying grace lost by sin, to deliver men out of the jaws of hell, and to set them at liberty of the sons of God, and to make them heirs of the heavenly kingdom, in fine, kings and princes, emperors and all sorts of men are liable and subject to their jurisdiction, and the priest alone can pronounce sentence of life or death against them. And is this not a good power? Is this not a power superior to all others; so that I don't wonder none of our adversaries think and say with the scribes

and pharisees (Luke 5:21) "who can forgive sins but God alone?" By which they will signify that it seems to be incredible, that God Almighty should have given such a power to men. But legitimate testimony of the holy fathers, the consent of Councils, the constant doctrine of the Roman Catholick infallible Church of God convinces us of the contrary.[46]

In the sixteenth century Martin Luther had come to the conclusion that the Christian is justified by faith alone, not by faith and good works, thereby laying the groundwork for one of the principal sources of divergence between Catholics and Protestants. In early eighteenth century Maryland, Henry Neale discussed this issue in a lengthy sermon "On Faith."

The opinion, or to speak more properly, the error of the modern Sectarys, is that faith alone justified us in the sight of God; that our good works, how perfect soever they may be, contribute nothing to salvation; that life everlasting is not given us by title of recompense, but by form of a simple inheritance which we cannot merit, of which we take possession without having acquired any right thereunto. Such is the language of heresy.[47]

Most of the preachers of eighteenth century Maryland dealt with heresy and error in abstract terms, cautious, no doubt, not to be too direct in their preaching and thereby attract the notice of their non-Catholic neighbors and perhaps stir up anti-Catholic sentiment. However, a few of the preachers were more polemical, naming names, and focusing on the heretics of the present time as inheritors of and disseminators of error. Any anonymous preacher of the period is typical of this style.

And in the annals of religion we read of only a few insignificant knots of Errorists who refused him divine honours. The system of these heretics, the spawn of Ebion, revived in the 16th century by Socinius, met with the reaction it merited as soon as its restless and anti-Christian professors had published their blasphemous tenets and is held in the utmost horror not only here but in that country where every other error is welcomed as to its own and natural asylum.[48]

A few preachers were actually bold enough to direct their remarks at the Protestants themselves. Henry Neale adopted this tactic in his sermon, "On Faith."

Ye have sown much and brought in little. Ye have eaten and were not filled; Ye drank and were not sated; ye have clothed and were not warmed: And he that got wages, put it into a bag with holes. And again, ye looked for much and lo! it came to little; and when ye brought it home, I blew upon it. Why! says the Lord of Hosts; because my house is deserted, and ye have run every man into his own house. As if he should say ye have abandoned the Church, which is my house, and made yourselves particular churches, every one according to his private fancy. Ye let yourselves be carryed away with every part of novelty. Ye hear preachers and doctors that I have not authorized and by a capricious, whimsical fickleness prefer their maxims and sentiments to the universal steady rule established by me. This is the worm that has marrd all your works.[49]

John Boone, speaking at Newtown in 1765, was even more direct in speaking to non-Catholics.

Here let me, in the bowels of Jesus Christ, the spouse of this his holy Catholic Church, here let me, I say, address myself to you, if any are here present, who have unhappily separated yourselves from her communion. Tell me, O my Christians. but mistaken Christians., why, O why have you thus forsaken and deserted her who first brought you forth to Christ and his Gospell. Why O why have you rent and tore the seamless coat of Christ your common Savior and Redeemer.

Speak boldly here, ye novelists, ye modern reformers of the Church's faith! Speak boldly and dare to say that Christ's promises are not to be relied on.[50]

While often attempting to be sensitive to the situation wherein Catholics found themselves in eighteenth century Maryland, the Jesuit preachers were nonetheless not afraid of the task of defending the faith both internally and externally to those who questioned it. Two simple lines from two different preachers sum up the apologetics of the Maryland Jesuits.

One thing more I have to recommend to you, which is constantly to believe what the Roman Catholick Church believes.[51]

The true and solid answer every Catholick ought to give when any point of his belief is called into question; my holy mother the Catholic Church has told me and all God has told to my mother the Church.[52]

CONCLUSION

As we come to the end of our study of the ecclesiology preached by eighteenth century Anglo-American Jesuits in the Maryland Mission, the obvious question which comes to mind is how successful were the preachers in conveying a sense of Church to their flocks, and in maintaining their somewhat isolated and buffeted flock within the communion of the Roman Catholic Church. To read Louis Roels' sermon for Sexagesima Sunday one would think that the Maryland Jesuits were complete failures in the art of preaching and religious persuasion.

> . . . You are a sort of Christians. who come indeed to a sermon yet they are not present, they see the preacher but they hear him not, because a thousand sinful thoughts withdraw their attention; tho their bodies are in the chapel, their thoughts are upon the ramble.[53]

Doubtless, Father Roels was using the type of homiletic rhetoric which every generation of preacher has employed to recover a congregation which occasionally wandered from the Sunday "entertainments." The evidence of history would seem to produce a much more positive conclusion about the Jesuit preaching.

Today, two centuries later, virtually all of the Jesuit chapels and Mass stations, including Newtown, Port Tobacco, Tuckahoe, and St. Inigoes, still function as parishes in Maryland. St. Thomas Manor at Port Tobacco is the oldest continuously occupied Jesuit residence in the world. Not only did the Catholics to whom they ministered remain faithful to the Church, but when the nascent American Church was ready to develope to the next level in the years after Independence, it was the Maryland Catholics who provided the seat of the first American diocese at Baltimore in 1789, and the first American bishop in the person of John Carroll. It is one of the few, if not the only example in the history of the Church where a missionary hierarchy was initially established by a native son. The diocese of Baltimore (raised to archdiocese in 1808) eventually gave rise to over 170 daughter sees across the United States.

Not only did Maryland provide America's first bishop, but the Maryland Catholics also provided the first lay leadership in individuals like Declaration of Independence signer Charles Carroll of Carrollton, Constitution signer Daniel Carroll, and Supreme Court Chief Justice Roger Brooke Taney. The earliest flowering of religious life in Anglo-America was at the Carmelite convent at Port Tobacco, deep in the heart of Maryland's Tidewater country. After the restoration of the Jesuits, the remaining fathers of the Maryland Mission gave rise to the Maryland Province. Today there are ten Jesuit provinces across the country with nearly five thousand members. Having been impressed with the education they received on the continent, it was these Maryland ex-Jesuits and Catholics who established the oldest enduring center of Catholic education in the new nation at Georgetown, which celebrated its bicentennial in 1989. Finally, when Maryland Catholics joined their fellow countrymen in the drive westward across the continent, they did not abandon their Catholic faith, but brought it with them. Even today, in the midst of largely Protestant rural Kentucky, there are three counties (Marion, Nelson, and Washington) known as the "Kentucky Holy Land," which were settled at the end of the eighteenth century by pioneers from Maryland coming through the Cumberland Gap, and they remain overwhelmingly Catholic to this day.[54]

From all the evidence it would appear that the isolated circuit-riding Jesuits of eighteenth century Maryland did in fact convey a real vision of ecclesiology to their colonial flock, and succeeded through their preaching in nourishing the beginnings of what would become the American Church.

Notes

1. Avery Dulles. *Models of the Church*. New York: Image Books, 1987.

2. The American Catholic Sermon Collection gathered in the Special Collections Division of Georgetown University's Lauinger Memorial Library consists of original eighteenth and nineteenth century Anglo-American Catholic sermons from three different collections, namely, Georgetown University, Woodstock College, and the Maryland Province of the Society of Jesus.

3. For a history of the Maryland Jesuits, see Thomas Hughes, *History of the Society of Jesus in North America: Colonial and Federal: Text*. 2 Vols. London: Longmans, Greene and Co., 1917.

4. Both Farmer and Manners anglicized their names on coming to America. Farmer's real name was Steinmeyer, and Manners' real name was Sittensperger.

5. For more information on Farmer, see John M. Daley, S.J. "Pioneer Missionary: Ferdinand Farmer, S.J. 1720–1786," *The Woodstock Letters* LIXXV (June 1946): 103–115; (October 1946): 207–231; (February 1947): 311–321.

6. John Tracy Ellis, *Catholics in Colonial America* (Baltimore: Helicon Press, 1963), p. 359.

7. For a summary of the political position of Maryland's Catholics, see Thomas O'Brien Hanley, *Their Rights and Liberties* (Chicago: Loyola Press, 1984).

8. John Tracy Ellis, ed., *Documents of American Catholic History* (Milwaukee: Bruce Publishing Co., 1962), p. 126.

9. Although there is some indication that the vicars apostolic of the London District in England had been given jurisdiction over the missions in America, this jurisdiction was never in fact exercised. Carroll was appointed superior on June 9, 1784.

10. Robert Emmett Curran, *American Jesuit Spirituality* (New York: Paulist Press, 1988), p. 14.

11. American Catholic Sermon Collection, Georgetown University Special Collections (hereafter ACSC), Nea-4.

12. John L. McKenzie, *Dictionary of the Bible* (Milwaukee: Bruce Publishing Co., 1962), p. 481.

13. ACSC, Car-3.

14. ACSC, Boo-1.
15. *Ibid.*
16. *Ibid.*
17. ACSC, Neal-2.
18. ACSC, Pi-5.
19. ACSC, Xb-5.
20. ACSC, Wi-3.
21. ACSC, Ro-9.
22. *Ibid.*
23. ACSC, Bi-6.
24. ACSC, Car-42.
25. ACSC, Bi-7.
26. ACSC, Bi-7.
27. ACSC, Car-13.
28. ACSC, Mos-8.
29. ACSC, Je-25.
30. ACSC, Boa-4.
31. ACSC, Di-23.
32. ACSC, Car-6.
33. ACSC, Mol-7.
34. ACSC, Se-21.
35. ACSC, Di-20.
36. ACSC, Hu-3.
37. Curran, P. 11.
38. ACSC, Mos-1.
39. ACSC, Pi-5.
40. ACSC, Mos-1.
41. ACSC, Ro-9.
42. ACSC, Pi-5. This is the only example I have found in the surveyed sermons where the Church of England, the dominant and established church in the colony, is actually mentioned by name.
43. ACSC, Di-14.
44. ACSC, Se-12.
45. ACSC, Je-10.
46. ACSC, Ma-1.
47. ACSC, Nea-4. Neale would seem to be on shaky theological ground himself when he speaks of justification as a right.
48. ACSC, Xb-5.

49. ACSC, Nea-4.
50. ACSC, Boo-1.
51. ACSC, Ca-5.
52. ACSC, Ro-9.
53. ACSC, Ro-19.
54. Clyde F. Crews, *An American Holy Land* (Wilmington: Michael Glazier, Inc., 1987), p. 36.

Marian Spirituality in Early America

Michael Sean Winters

When John Carroll, first bishop and archbishop of Baltimore, was called upon to place his new diocese under the
protection of a heavenly patron, he choose Mary the
Mother of God, and the first cathedral church built in the
United States he named the Cathedral of the Assumption.
It might well strike the contemporary surveyor of those
early days of Catholicism in the new republic as odd that
Carroll, a man keenly aware of the latent prejudice and
easily disturbed sensitivities of the Protestant majority,
would so invoke the Blessed Virgin Mary whose cult was
so distinctively and peculiarly Catholic. But if Carroll was
a man of his age, he was more so a man of his creed, and
neither he nor his fellow clergy were prepared to diminish
the role of Mary in the life of Jesus, in the economy of
salvation nor in the devotion of the Church.

Though it is hoped one day that some scholar will under-
take a study of the beginnings of devotion to the Blessed
Mother in the Catholic Church of the United States, the
present author sets a less ambitious task, namely, to survey
those sermons that treat of Mary found among the American Catholic Sermon Collection.[1] This collection is fortui-
tous, not comprehensive, and so we cannot hope to attain
a well-rounded picture of as multi-faceted a phenomenon
as Marian piety. But a careful analysis of these texts will

permit us to gain some insight as to how these early American priests instructed their flocks on these distinctively Catholic doctrines and devotions.

The earliest dated sermon here considered is that given by Father John Lewis in 1750 on the Incarnation, although the discourse given by Fr. Attwood on the same subject is apparently a revised translation of a French text and might date from as early as the first decade of the eighteenth century.[2] The latest dated sermon is that of John-Baptist Diderich in 1787 although the short sermon of John Carroll here included might well have been delivered at a later date. Some of the sermons considered treat specifically of the Blessed Mother, most treating of her Assumption. Also examined have been those sermons in the collection that deal with the saints in general, the Incarnation and Nativity of Christ, and his Passion as well.

All of the preachers whose sermons are here surveyed were members of the Maryland Mission of the Society of Jesus. After the suppression of that same Society in 1773, these men stayed at their ministerial labors in the British colonies and constituted the early clergy of the infant republic's middle colonies. Although what Catholics there were in the United States were largely concentrated in Maryland and Pennsylvania, even here they represented but the smallest of minorities in an overwhelmingly Protestant milieu. They lacked even the semblance of the ecclesiastical organizational structures that characterized the Catholic Church of that age, there being no resident episcopal authority until Carroll's appointment in 1789.

But preach these Jesuits and ex-Jesuits did, despite their many hardships, and their sermons reflect the broad learning of their European education and training. The lack of any mature ecclesiastical organization was not mirrored by any corresponding poverty of doctrinal soundness or eloquence. And, in the matter at hand, there is clearly no want of devotion nor misunderstanding of doctrine as regards the Blessed Mother of Jesus Christ.

MARY IN THE LIFE OF JESUS

Perhaps the most surprising feature of the sermons is the relative absence of the Blessed Mother from the sermons that treat of the life of Jesus. John Boarman's sermon on the nativity of Jesus[3] and as well the sermon of John Bolton on the same subject[4] completely omit any reference to the Blessed Mother. The former's notes for a separate Nativity sermon include only the following plea to the Virgin:

> Assist us O glorious Virgin by your intercession with thy Blessed Son, that as thou was made worthy to conceive and bring forth this Great Redeemer of mankind so we by his mercy and your powerful prayers may be also made worthy to receive him at his coming into the world. *Ave Maria.*[5]

What does impress one about the Nativity accounts is the ease with which the preachers expressed themselves in the most intimate terms about Jesus Christ himself. The focus is each and every time on Jesus' condition of poverty and powerlessness at birth, as in contrast to his powerful intercessory role and merciful judgement. There is little role assigned to Mary at all in these accounts which is especially ironic when, as we shall see, Mary is given great prominence in those sermons that treat the Incarnation as a soteriological fact rather than as an historical one.

Similarly, the few sermons that discuss the passion of Christ give almost no role to the Blessed Mother. Father Jenkins' Passion sermon asks what the Lord sees from the cross and answers his own question thus, "On both sides of him, 2 malefactors crucified with him, at his feet Mary that so tender, beloved mother, fainting and dying away.''[6] That is all: Mary and the malefactors. Though Mary is seen as present at the crucifixion, a view not shared by the synoptic evangelists, there is no lengthy tribute to Mary at the foot of the Cross here.

MARY IN THE ECONOMY OF SALVATION

Two of Father Lewis' sermons, one on the Incarnation and the other on the Purification in the Temple, set forth most clearly the role of Mary in the economy of salvation. Although Lewis, and indeed all the preachers surveyed, would say that Mary's role is essentially to give birth, they all see that merely as the historical source of a role which has much greater diversity and complexity.

In his 1750 Incarnation sermon, Lewis cites the nativity account at some length to portray Mary and Joseph as links between the Covenant of Israel and the New Covenant of Christ.[7] But at the same time as he is connecting the two epochs of salvation history, he sees Mary's labor and giving birth as the first sign of a distinction between the two, citing Augustine to the effect that ''as she conceived without sin so she brought forth without pain . . . that unhappy sentence pronounced against Eve & the descendents of her sex: You shall bring forth your children in pain; was reversed in her because she was delivered of Christ with pleasure.''[8] Lewis further notes that Mary's virginity had to be maintained for carnal conception is the conduit of Adam's sin. He concludes his treatment of Mary's role in the Incarnation with a testament to Mary's perpetual virginity.[9]

In his Purification sermon, Lewis is again at pains to link the early life of Christ with his Jewish heritage and the promises of Israel, noting the purification of Mary, though unnecessary because of her virgin state, was in accordance with the Law of Moses citing Leviticus 12:6.[10] He then proceeds to delineate five graces or favors that were bestowed upon Mary as corrolaries to her conception of Jesus:

> The first extraordinary grace then bestowed upon her was her being elected, from all eternity to be the mother of God . . . for by virtue of this election, she was chosen to be, next after Christ, the principal instrument of man's redemption: by virtue of the same she was chosen to be, by the nearest relation a pure creature is capable of, the immaculate spouse of God the Father . . . Hence flows the second extraordinary favour bestowed upon her, her being sanctified in her mother's womb in the very moment of her conception for which reason she is the only saint upon earth, whose conception and nativity is solemnized in the Church by a particular feast. . . . Whence also flows the 3d extraordinary favour: of her having been preserved throughout the course of her life from all spot or stain of actual sin . . . [Her fourth extraordinary grace was] her being overshadowed by the power and virtue of the Holy Ghost; and so remaining a pure Virgin, at the same time that she became the true and natural mother of God . . . I pass over the rest of her life, whereof thirty years where [sic] spent in the company of Jesus: and all passed in an uninterrupted practice of the sublimest virtues & a continual increase of grace & merits, till God was pleased to crown them with the last singular favour, I mean, that of her glorious asumption into heaven.[11]

This excerpt illustrates an explanation of Mary's role in the economy of salvation from the singular historical event of the birth of Jesus to a role of cosmic proportions, extending from the beginning to the end of time. That Lewis would easily "pass over the rest of her life" is of course necessary due to the dearth of treatment Mary receives in the New Testament. But his willingness to assign Mary a cosmic role illustrates the Church's on-going development of Marian doctrine which he himself proposes as evidence for the singularity of the conception of Mary.

While Lewis' sermon is the most detailed in drawing out the Marian implications of the conception of Jesus, the vast majority of the sermons in the collection that treat of Mary are those in commemoration of her Assumption. John-Baptist Diderich, in offering evidence for the Assumption queries:

> God preserved her from all sin; conserved her always a virgin, being a mother, preserved her from pain, when she brought forth, and when she died: when then should he not preserve her from the corruption of her body?[12]

Diderich further relates the extent of her exultation to the extent of her own humility: "we need not doubt, but God has exalted her in proportion to her humility; and that as she reputed herself the lowest of all, he, who regarded her humility, has raised her above all."[13]

If Diderich's exposition on the Assumption is somewhat restrained in its flights of honorifics, the same cannot be said for Father John Bolton whose discourse on the Assumption reaches the high water mark of high Mariology:

> It being to day the feast of the Virgin's assumption, no doubt, Christians, you expect I should say something in praise of this glorious queen, the world's empress and mother to no less a person than a God incarnate . . . And as it is incomparable which she bore, ineffable which she conceived, so certainly must be inconceivable the reward of her eternal greatness. What tongue

than shall we find able to declare and what mind sufficient to comprehend and what human understanding able to express with what joy, jubily and content, the degrees of celestial souls go forth to meet their queen and empress; with what splendour they present her to the throne of glory, and with what divine embraces she was received by her son and exalted above all creatures according to her worth and merit. Hence it is that St. Peter Damian sticks not to affirm that this assumption of our Lady was far more stately, glorious and set out with greater promp, than was the ascension of Christ our Saviour; and alledges this pious and forceable reason, that in the ascension of Christ his concomitancy was only made up of pious souls and angels; But in the assumption of our Virgin not only saints and angels, but the king both of saints and angels, the Sun of justice, the God of majesty, the Prince of Glory whose dignity is infinite, whose immensity unmeasurable and whose greatness is boundless, came forth in company of all just souls, angels, and the court of heaven to conduct her to the Eternal Father as his daughter, to welcome her as his mother and present her to the Holy Ghost as his spouse and darling.[14]

But Bolton's purpose in enunciating such exalted claims is not mere verbal puffery, for the second portion of his sermon is dedicated to presenting Mary as the mediator and model for Christians. Mary is seen as the *Regina caeli* but she, too, is queen of our *Salve Regina*. Her proximity to the Lord in heaven is claimed to be a boon for sinners who now have "an advocate who knows how to deal both suppliantly and efficaciously the affairs of our security being as well the judge's mother as mother of mercy."[15]

Father Attwood follows the same motif, but in astonishingly intimate phraseology, commenting that Mary is, a mediatrix, and advocate to God. Jesus Christ presents his wounds to the Eternal Father, which are so many mouths that plead in our behalf, the mother presents her breasts to her Son in our favour, the eternal Father can refuse nothing to this son, this son can refuse nothing to his mother. Ah never let us limite her power with god, let us not judge it ill that she showers down so many graces on sinners and impenitants.[16]

John Carroll likewise attests to the high Mariology of the day and ties in Mary's role as advocate with her exalted status in heaven:

Not only her blessed and pure soul was carried into heaven, but according to the general persuasion of pious Christians, a persuasion derived from the earliest ages of the Church, her unsullied body in union with her soul, was raised and introduced into the mansions of everlasting life. Today, dear Christians, let us pour forth our hearty congratulations for the exalted honour to which she is elevated; let us rejoice, that she is so glorified; and at the same time let us remember that we have thereby obtained a powerful, a tender, a willing patroness and advocate at the tribunal of divine justice.[17]

In each of these passages, the tension between Mary's cosmic exaltation and her approachability is resolved by reference to her role as mediator for Christians with her son Jesus Christ. Thus, while she is portrayed as exalted above all creatures, this makes her all the more likely as a candidate for devotion by the faithful, for the more surely will her prayers be answered. The corrolation noted between the extent of her humility and the extent of her glorification makes this devotion all the more sensible.

MARY IN THE LIFE OF THE CHURCH

On the Feast of the Assumption in 1780, John Bolton mounted the pulpit to preach on devotion to the Blessed Mother and began,

> As the church celebrates to day the feast of the Assumption of the Blessed Virgin, it would not be improper to speak of some devotions to her, and see what are the exceptions against them, and what the abuses in them. And of all these whatever they be, we lay down this as a general ground for coming to a good understanding, that none of them, however approved, are enjoined by the Church and so far from being made a term of communion, that all the members of it are at full liberty of using them if they think fit, and likewise of letting them alone.[18]

Of course, it is impossible to know whether the apologetics he offered for Marian devotion were the result of any specific charges made against the Church's practice or whether his recital of these was merely rhetorical. In either event, his congregation received a lengthy dissertation on the rightness of devotion to the Blessed Mother and on how such devotion could be rightly made.

Bolton noted the great advantage of the Rosary for those deprived of the higher religious sensibilities of the educated, "and what this advantage is, those may easily imagine, who know how dull and barren are the minds of the unlearned, and how soon they are at a stand when they even intend to turn their hearts to God."[19] He then cites and refutes the charge that those who pray the beads pray ten times more to Mary than they do to God,

> Because when I desire the Blessed Virgin to pray to God for me, I in this acknowledge, that all is in the

hands of God, that all must come from him, that he is the fountain of all good; and in asking the Virgin Mary to pray to him for me is only owning her a creature, desiring her to be petitioner with me, and consequently acknowledging, that God's gifts are not in hers, but in his own hands . . . for all that I ask of her, is to be petitioner to God for me, and here my prayer is as much directed to God as my petition is to the king when I desire another to deliver it to him and to make an interest for me.[20]

Bolton further notes that praying to Mary does not connote greater confidence in her than in God but, rather, greater confidence in the efficacy of her prayers than in our own. He also replies to those that question the force of repitition in the Rosary with his own query, "if the prayer be good, where can be the harm of repeating it? Can persons in distress be reproved for often calling for help?"[21]

In discussing the Sodalities and Confraternities dedicated to the Blessed Virgin, Bolton urges them to avoid the temptation of thinking that such devotions will save them if they do not follow her pious example in life, "we ought to entertain no hopes of salvation, whatever our devotion to the Blessed Virgin and the saints, if we do not repent of our sins, as God has ordained and quit our evil ways, to live such true Christians as the Gospel requires."[22] Bolton also sees a proper understanding of right devotion to the Blessed Mother as essential to restoring the unity of the Christian Church: "And as for all abuses either of ignorance or design, we are as much at liberty in denouncing or condemning them, as those who are not of our communion, and therefore without reason make these the plea for their separation."[23]

Twelve years prior to Bolton's sermon cited above, Father Lewis finished his sermon on the Feast of the Purification with a treatment of devotions to the Blessed Mother.

He commended his congregation to the practice of three devotions specifically. First, "never to begin or end the day without putting ourselves under the protection of the Blessed Virgin, by saying some short prayer in honour of her: for we must all regard her as our mother in Jesus Christ."[24] Second he urged them to "devout observance of the feasts ordained in honour of her," commenting that as at a king's court on solemn days one wears "rich new cloaths . . . [o]ur old cloaths, therefore, that is our old habits of sin, will suit very ill with the solemnity"[25] of the Marian feast days. Lastly, he commends the Rosary to his flock and, like Bolton after him, Lewis answers the charges that repitition deadens the mind and that the Rosary results in praying to Mary ten times more frequently than to God. Here, it is the repititive pleas of a beggar that are used to remove reproof and Lewis also cites the example of a petition to a king delivered by another's hand to refute the latter charge.[26] Finally, he refutes those opposed to Marian devotions in more general terms that implicitly invoke Mary as a model of Christian humility as well:

If they who blame us for [our devotions to Mary], either think her not charitable enough to interest herself in our behalf, or not powerful enough to obtain anything for us, or perhaps think themselves to have as good an interest with Christ as the Blessed Virgin, his Mother, let us at least be far from entertaining either so mean an opinion of her, or so proud a one of ourselves.[27]

Thus, Mary's dual role as protectrine and paradigm of Christian virtue are here joined, but it is to the latter that we must now attend.

In his sermon on the veneration due to saints, Bolton makes the following general observation:

> Let us again take notice that to honour the Saints and
> reverence their images as thereby resembled and rep-
> resented to us as we ought, we must be trying to
> imitate their virtues, laying before us their holy lives
> for a sample and pattern, to copy after, this must be
> our only intent, the only fruit we are to propose to
> ourselves in honouring them.[28]

Having already established that the reverence of the saints
must be directed to God, the preacher is here communicating to his hearers that the adoration of the saints will also
be in vain unless the virtues which so distinguished the
saints as friends of God, are mirrored in their own lives.
This applies as well to the Blessed Mother as it does to any
of the saints.

Because most of the sermons, as stated above, premise
the glories of Mary upon her role in the Incarnation and
several take the *Magnificat* for their text, it is to be expected that of all the virtues ascribed to the Virgin Mother,
humility has the most prominent place. Thus we find John
Carroll's sermon on the Assumption commencing with this
observation based on the above mentioned text,

> In these words did the Blessed Virgin, whose glorious
> assumption we this day keep, acknowledge the mercies
> of God to her, and humbly confess that the great
> privileges bestowed on her were the effects of his
> gracious and all bountiful providence over her. She did
> not presume to attribute them to her own deserts.[29]

Carroll's words reinforce the twin concepts that adoration
of the saints must be related to God and that it is Mary's
humility which so commenced her to the reception of
Christian dignity.

This dual theme is likewise enunciated by Father Attwood in his already quoted sermon, but he goes on to point

out other virtues which the Virgin possessed which call for emulation.

> She is in the midst of graces, an Angel salutes her, and says that she is filled therewith; yet she anihilates herself, she is employed only in her nothingness, she confesses god beholds nothing in this mistery but the lowliness of his servant, *q*[ui]*a respescit humilitatem.* Yet she is so much taken up with her baseness that in the time when she was to be raised, she seems to make some resistance, in saying she was nothing but the handmaid of him whose mother she was to be. *Ecce Ancilla domi*[ni]. Where shall we find nowadays, such humble sentiments? Have we humility whilst we run after greatness? Whilst in all things we seek nothing but glory? Whilst the best advantage of witt, of beauty of eloquence, so much pass and swell our hearts, as if they were the greatest goods, and whilst we joyn to that haughty ingratitude a contempt of Eternal goods, the Blessed Virgin is so pure, and chast that alto' an angel comes to announce the conception of God in her bowels, she would not consent to the honour without the Angel assured her it woud be without the loss of her virginity.[30]

Chastity and purity have been added to the list of virtues worthy of emulation here. Attwood also reinforces the vanity of devotion to the Blessed Mother without imitation of her virtues warning that she will "disown you for her children."

Father Bolton adds obedience and faithfulness to the list, seeing these as necessary corrolaries of humility:

> Thus we have considered Mary raised to a most eminent degree of glory; we admired her, then glorified, yet it must not be absolutely and precisely because she

was the Mother of God, but because she had been
obedient and faithful to God, because she had been
humble in the sight of God and by reason of these two
qualities had render'd herself in a singular manner and
by excellence the handmaid of God and arrived at so
elevated a degree of happiness.[31]

This text departs a little from the earlier ones in setting
Mary's eminence as derivative of her virtues and in distinction from the grace of being the Mother of God. As mentioned above, Bolton's sermon is the most filled with sump-
tuous phraseology and praise of Mary of any surveyed, and
he is certainly not intending to portray Mary as a distinct
source of grace. But it is just such a blurring of distinctions
in the ambition of heaping praise upon the Blessed Mother
that was bound to arouse the interest of non-Catholic
Christians, who thought the Catholic Church was commit-
ting idolatry in its devotion to the Blessed Mother.

John Carroll not only saw Mary as a model of Christian
virtues, but likewise as a paradigm for certain truths of the
faith:

Above all, let us constantly bear in mind the holy and
virtuous examples left us by her in this life, if we wish
to enjoy a share of her happiness in the next: For the
present, I wish to confine your attention to these two
circumstances of her life; first, that the dignity, which
Mary derived from the sanctifying grace bestowed on
her at the moment of her conception, in consideration
of her future dignity of Mother of God, discovers to us
the great excellency of the grace of adoption and
reconciliation bestowed on us thro the means of the
sacraments of baptism, and pennance; and secondly,
that the fidelity of Mary to that first grace teaches us
our indispensable obligation of using our earnest en-

deavour to preserve the grace of justification conferred
on us in either of the abovementioned sacraments.[32]

Carroll explains that the greatness of the first grace must
be seen vis-a-vis the greatness of the evil which is original
sin. The rest of the text is not extant, but one can follow
the logic of this extract to conclude how advanced Carroll
was in his understanding of the richness of Mary as a model
for the sacramental life of the Church. Just as Mary was
necessarily free from the stain of original sin in order that
she might bear the Saviour, it is only through the cleansing
waters of baptism, and the regenerative effects of penance
that we can be admitted to the reception of Christ in the
Eucharist. Mary is thus not merely a model for individual
Christians by way of virtue but is a paradigm for the Church
herself.

Another common feature of these sermons that is illustra-
tive of Marian devotion, is the practice of concluding the
introductory paragraph of their sermons by having the
congregation recite in unison the *Hail Mary*. This is a
tradition which was carried over even into the youthful
memories of the present writer. No explanation of the
origin of this practice could be found but it is a commonplace in the sermons surveyed.

CONCLUSIONS

The text of the fifth session of the first Synod of Baltimore, convoked by the newly elected and consecrated
Bishop Carroll in 1791, states:

At the beginning of our episcopate, we have been
impelled by an ardent desire to make the Blessed
Virgin Mary the principal patroness of our diocese, so
that by Her intercession, faith and love of God and

sanctity of life in the people committed to our care
may flourish and increase more and more. We were
consecrated first Bishop of Baltimore on the feast of
the Assumption and we are led to honour Her as our
patron and we exhort our venerable colleagues to
venerate Her with a great devotion and often and
zealously commend this devotion to their flock, so that
in Her powerful patronage they may rely on Her protection from all harm.[33]

It is obvious from the sermons surveyed that the prominent
role Mary has played in the spirituality of the Catholic
Church of the United States was not a nineteenth century
import, part and parcel of the immigrant wave, but rather
that this prominence is found in the colonial Anglo-American Catholic Church as well. Devotions to the Blessed
Mother such as the Rosary were commonplace and Marian
sodalities were already organized. The faithful were referred to the efficacy of images of the Blessed Mother and
the saints for stirring up in their hearts a proper sense of
devotion. This devotion to the Mother of God was further
presented as something that distinguished Catholics from
other Christians to the credit of the former. She was being
presented in sermons as a model of virtue for the emulation
of individual Catholics and, at least in the case of John
Carroll, as a model for the sacramental life of the Church.

Also obvious is the fact that this devotion, and specifically its distinctively Catholic qualities, was a source of
some controversy especially to non-Catholics. The defen-
siveness of some of the apologia for devotion to the Virgin
Mary is pronounced and preachers warned their flocks not
to go further than the Church allowed by way of excess in
Marian devotion. But that they defended such devotion as
was theologically sound, there can be no doubt. Carroll's
dedication of his new cathedral to the patronage of Mary
under the title of the Assumption can be seen, therefore,

not as an anomalistic event in the age of the Enlightenment, but as a due recognition of the traditional role of Mary in the life of the Universal Church and of the already pronounced devotion to the Mother of God among the American Catholics whose cathedral it was.

Notes

1. The American Catholic Sermon Collection is located in the Special Collections Division of the Mark Lauinger Library. Georgetown University, Washington, D.C. The collection brings together sermons from the archives of Woodstock College, the Maryland province of the Society of Jesus and Georgetown University. The sermons have been assigned catalogue numbers by the archivist which numbers are used here in providing references.

2. Robert Emmet Curran, S.J., ed. *American Jesuit Spirituality: The Maryland Tradition, 1634–1900.* (New York: Paulist Press, 1987), p. 78.

3. John Boarman, American Catholic Sermon Collection, Special Collections, Mark Lauinger Library, Georgetown University, Washington, D.C. (Hereafter, ACSC), Boa-7.

4. ACSC, Bol-19.

5. ACSC, Boa-13.

6. ACSC, Je-16.

7. ACSC, Le-1.

8. Ibid.

9. Ibid.

10. ACSC, Le-13.

11. Ibid.

12. ACSC, Di-30.

13. Ibid.

14. ACSC, Bol-1.

15. Ibid.

16. ACSC, At-1.

17. ACSC, Car-29.

18. ACSC, Bol-9.

19. Ibid.

20. Ibid.

21. Ibid.

22. Ibid.

23. Ibid.

24. ACSC, Le-13.

25. Ibid.

26. Ibid.

27. Ibid.

28. ACSC, Bol-8.

29. ACSC, Car-29.

30. ACSC, At-1.

31. ACSC, Bol-1.

32. ACSC, Car-29.

33. Peter Guilday. *A History of the Councils of Baltimore*. (New York: The Macmillan Company, 1932), p. 68.

John Carroll and the Enlightenment

Carla Bang

Although the Maryland Colonial Assembly passed a law granting religious freedom to all Christians by 1649, in the early eighteenth-century it had enacted the most rigorous anti-Catholic legislation in America. These laws forbade the public celebration of Mass and the imparting of a Catholic education. Furthermore, these same laws stripped Catholics of the right to vote or to hold public office. Nevertheless, while these laws were strict, wealthy Catholics could avoid some of their consequences. Catholic education was carried out secretly in Catholic manor houses or in small local schools supported by parents while sporadic attempts to organize secondary education, as represented by a Jesuit school at Bohemia on Maryland's upper Eastern Shore, were initiated as well.

One early beneficiary of this educational effort was John Carroll, the son of wealthy Anglo-Irish parents, who received his first formal schooling at the Jesuit institution in Bohemia when he was twelve years old.[1] In 1748, after two years of study at Bohemia Manor Academy, Carroll continued his education at St. Omer College, founded in 1582 by Robert Parsons, an English Jesuit. St. Omer was long favored by Anglo-American Catholic colonists as the site for the continued education of their children. When England's penal Laws suppressed Catholic education in that country, some Catholic schools relocated to the European Continent, remaining essentially English in character and spartan in orientation, while permitting English and American families to continue the tradition of Catholic education for their children. After several years at St. Omer, John Carroll, responding to his vocation to the Jesuits, entered the novitiate in 1753 at nearby Watten, Flanders. From Watten, he went to the Jesuit College in Liège to study philosophy as a Jesuit scholastic in 1757. Having finished these studies Carroll taught philosophy at Liège for four years until he began his own theological studies there in 1765. Carroll was ordained four years later, a particularly difficult time for the Society of Jesus which was being expelled from Portugal, France, and Spain, as well as from Naples and Sicily, mostly for political reasons. After ordination, Carroll took up his final teaching assignment at the Jesuit college in Bruges, Flanders.

In 1771, Carroll made his final profession as a Jesuit and a few months later began a tour of central Europe which lasted until 1773. This tour broadened Carroll's horizons, since up to this time his knowledge of the Continent had been confined to the cities in Flanders where he had studied and taught in English colleges. With the dissolution of the Jesuits by Clement XIV in 1773, Carroll returned to his mother's house at Rock Creek, Maryland, the following year. While living with his mother, he tended to the spiritual needs of Catholic families in nearby Maryland and Virginia.

Carroll was part of a family which would play an influential role in the colonial struggle for independence. Charles Carroll of Carrollton, John Carroll's cousin, would sign the Declaration of Independence, while Daniel, John's older brother, signed the Constitution on behalf of the State of Maryland.

Shortly after the opening of the American Revolution in April of 1776, Carroll accompanied his cousin Charles, and

Benjamin Franklin on a diplomatic mission to Canada. During this mission, Carroll formed a warm friendship with Franklin. Consequently, when Rome was considering an American superior for the Catholic clergy in the United States in 1784, Franklin, who was again on a diplomatic mission, this time in Paris, suggested that Carroll would be the most appropriate choice. The appointment was made and six years later, Carroll was consecrated bishop of Baltimore, the first Catholic diocese in the United States. In 1808 Baltimore was raised to metropolitan status which made Carroll archbishop over the sees of Philadelphia, New York, Boston and Bardstown, Kentucky. Upon his death in 1815, John Carroll left a firmly established Catholic church as a legacy to the growing republic.

Carroll lived during a particularly tumultuous philosophical era. The Enlightenment, the intellectual revolution in philosophy which began in England in the late seventeenth-century and quickly spread into the other European countries and America, reached its climax during the eighteenth-century in France. Few other movements in history have had such a profound effect on molding people's thoughts and shaping their actions. Lately, some modern scholars have maintained that John Carroll was influenced to a greater or lesser degree by the thinking of Enlightenment *philosophes*.[2] Such an assumption is not unreasonable considering that twenty-six years of Carroll's life had been spent in Europe, where he studied, taught, and traveled during the height of the Enlightenment's influence. In addition, Carroll and those members of his immediate family who were leaders of the young American Republic were contemporaries of men such as Thomas Jefferson, Benjamin Franklin, and Thomas Paine, all of whom were essentially deist in their outlook. An examination of Carroll's piety, teaching, and exhortations as manifested in his sermons, however, shows that he was not influenced by prevailing currents of Enlightenment thought.[3]

Although the intensity of the Enlightenment's impact varied from country to country and from one *philosophe* to another, the following significant revolutionary concepts commonly characterized the movement: that natural reason, unaided by revelation, held a pre-eminent place as the ultimate standard of truth and morality; that God was an impersonal supreme being who did not interfere with the workings of the universe after having created it and set it in motion; that man possessed the potential for infinite personal and social perfectibility because his nature was uncorrupted by original sin and autonomous reason was infallible; that there existed a single natural universal religion which could be known by man's use of his reason alone; and that Christianity was a form of superstitious priestcraft whose tyranny shackled man's freedom to think for himself. An analysis of Carroll's sermons not only shows no trace of these concepts, but rather, reveals that he held quite the opposite view.

I. THE PRE-EMINENCE OF REASON

The supremacy of reason in Enlightenment thought is well exemplified by the argument of the English philosopher, John Locke (1632–1704), who stated that "Reason must be our best judge and guide in every thing." Reason, he claimed, provides for the existence of God with a force ". . . equal to mathematical certainty." According to Locke, anything contrary to reason had to be rejected, regardless of the claims of religious authority. The Bible, for example, needed to be purged of all that was not in harmony with natural reason and of everything not directly dealing with morality.[4] Through this claim, Locke clearly established reason as the only infallible guide to truth. The norms of the Bible acceptable to Enlightenment man were only those which, in his view, were in consonance with reason and rational morality.

Isaac Newton (1642–1727), Locke's famous contemporary, confessed the existence of a God of nature, a God of the whole universe, but he could not believe that the truth about that God had been revealed only through Christ: "There is but one law for all nations, the law of righteousness and charity, dictated to the Christians by Christ, to the Jews by Moses, and to all mankind by the light of reason, and by this law all men are to be judged at the last day."[5] Thus Newton also proclaimed the supremacy of reason over revelation, denying the authority of Scripture and the historical claims of Christianity.

When confronted by a magnificent sunrise, the French deist, Voltaire (1694–1778), knelt and exclaimed, "I believe! I believe in you! Powerful God I believe! As for monsieur the Son and madame His Mother, that's a different story."[6] For Voltaire there was sufficient evidence of God's existence in nature; there was no need for the Bible. Characteristically, Voltaire doubted the traditional doctrine of the Church.

Thomas Paine (1737–1809), whose thought was influential on both sides of the Atlantic, in his *The Age of Reason* held that God is the creator and the author of moral law in the universe, that people had to obey that moral law, and that breaking it brought punishment. One who followed the moral law would discover the kindness and goodness of God, known directly in nature. Paine ridiculed the beliefs and institutions of revealed religion as nothing more than superstition. The Bible, Paine maintained, degraded human dignity since it depicted the Deity as cruel and capricious.[7] Deism, for Paine, was the victory of rational-natural morality over the superstitious dogma of revealed religion. Actions harmonious with nature and reason constituted virtue.

Like Voltaire and Paine, the majority of *philosophes* were

deists. They distrusted the religious authority and doctrines of churches and held that the existence of God and the duties of man were known by human reason alone, apart from supernatural revelation. Deists, therefore, accepted the existence of God and the necessity of leading a moral life purely on rational grounds.

The ultimate expression of the Enlightenment ideal of personal autonomy is well represented in Immanuel Kant's (1724–1804) *"Was ist Aufklärung?"* as:

> . . . Man's release from self-imposed tutelage. Tutelage is the inability to use one's natural powers without direction from another. This tutelage is called "self-imposed" because its cause is not any absence of rational competence but simply a lack of courage and resolution to use one's reason without direction from another. *Sapere aude!*—Dare to reason! Have the courage to use your own minds!—is the motto of enlightenment.[8]

Self-dependence—autonomy of intellect and emancipation from everything that interferes with one's independence—constituted another ideal of the Enlightenment.

Were Carroll's thoughts in harmony with or opposed to the thoughts of Enlightenment thinkers? That is, is reason, apart from revelation, all-sufficient for knowing the existence of God and necessary moral principles? Was Carroll an "Enlightenment thinker"?

According to Carroll, man's reason is liable to be blinded by passion and weakness of understanding; therefore, one cannot even know with certainty the "fundamental articles of religion," i.e., the existence of an "infinitely good" and "infinitely just" supreme being, and a state of after-life existence, in which a supreme being will confer reward and punishment according to one's performance in this life. Carroll argued that even the wisest and most talented individual who is favored with leisure and education cannot consistently pursue virtue while rejecting vice. He further maintained that without the guidance of revelation there is no sufficient foundation to support a person when doubt and uncertainty creep into his life. (pp. 377–380)[9] Carroll held that good examples of the ignorance and corruption to which human reason and human nature are prone can be found in the wisest philosophers in history: Socrates, Hume, and Voltaire, all of whom the deists venerated. On this point Carroll observed,

> Reflecting farther on that subject, I have thought it advisable and likely to produce many beneficial effects, to treat it more particularly, that you may be more convinced of the imperfections of the human understanding, and the need it has of being informed and enlightened by the splendor of divine revelation. . . . Socrates universally esteemed as the wisest of the heathen world . . . affords us nevertheless a memorable instance of the darkness in which human reason, unassisted by revelation, leaves the mind involved. . . . for after many sublime speculations and discourses on the nature and immortality of the human soul, his very last words are expressive of the greatest uncertainty respecting this very point. (pp. 375, 379–380)

Because of their uncertainty and ignorance of God's goodness and justice, even the wisest philosophers became discouraged and gave up their efforts to pursue virtue. According to Carroll this occurred because of

> . . . the imperfection of the human understanding, and its insufficiency to guide us, not only in all points concerning the doctrines and precepts of religion, but even in those which form, as it were, the very elements and first principles of faith and morality. (p. 375)

The first principles of faith and morality, explained Carroll, are

> . . . that there is a Supreme Being, the arbiter and disposer of all human things, who commands justice, truth and mutual love of one for the other; and that there is a state of existence after this life, in which the supreme Being will dispense rewards and punishments, according to each man's deserts. (p. 377)

Only by supernatural revelation, Carroll insisted, could the imperfections of human reason be compensated; ultimately, one gained the necessary knowledge in order to honor God as well as the way to learn correct morality. As Carroll argued,

> They [deists] think and assert that these points are sufficiently known and enforced by the natural lights of reason alone . . . whereas . . . unless the additional authority of God's word come in aid of the weakness of our understandings, mankind, in general, cannot acquire such a certainty of these fundamental articles of religion, as will be sufficient to insure their obedience and support their hopes. (p. 377)

The Gospel is divine revelation; it sheds light on all necessary truths and proper morality. (p. 385) Christians have the advantage of ". . . knowing a sovereign Judge of the living & the dead" and these considerations should keep them attached to their duty to keep the holy law of God. (pp. 455, 456) Carroll claimed that

> Unless you be intimately convinced of the existence of religion, and your obligation to believe it, and submit to its laws, the lessons of morality can have no hold on

your hearts . . . divine revelation is necessary to make known to mankind, with sufficient clearness, and establish upon sufficient authority, even some of the first principles of the law of nature, and secondly, that the law of nature, as far as it is discoverable by power of human reason alone, leaves us ignorant of, and uncertain in many points of our duty to God, on which our happiness essentially depends. (p. 376)

Hence, only divine revelation can compensate what is lacking in the natural powers of human reason. When divine revelation enlightens the human understanding, only then does one discover sufficiently the necessity of honoring the true and holy God, only then does one understand the scope of one's duties, and the end for which one is created. The Gospel, divine revelation, is the "word of God"—the word of "infinite holiness" and "infallible Truth." (pp. 386, 395) Hence, ". . . it should be heard with the greatest reverence; received with the greatest submission; & cherished by the most assiduous cultivation." (p. 395) Carroll declared that Christian revelation teaches that ". . . each of us, at our departure out of this world, will receive a sentence of mercy or condemnation from our Sovereign Judge." (p. 391) And it is Christian revelation that ". . . offers her aid, her more persuasive motives, and all her powerful sanctions to strengthen the dictates of nature." (p. 447) Carroll's insistence on the necessity of divine revelation in order to know truth and morality, and to sustain the motivation to pursue them is in direct opposition to the tenets of the Enlightenment thinkers who believed that natural morality, i. e., the law of nature, is sufficiently known by reason alone. Thus did Carroll, in his thought and preaching, override that of the Enlightenment proponents of the supremacy of natural reason over revelation.

II. THE IMPERSONALITY OF GOD

Many Enlightenment thinkers did not rule out the existence of a Supreme Being but they deprived him of the power to direct the course of the universe and the affairs of individuals. With his mechanical interpretation of the universe, Newton had a profound influence on the whole Enlightenment movement. He believed that God in his perfection had created a universal law that required no tinkering.[10] Since God was a perfect "watchmaker," men lived in a world where events moved as automatically as the ticking of a clock. Gone was the conception of a loving Providence directing the universe. Since, according to Enlightenment thinkers, God does not interfere with the world, miracles and grace were denied. Thomas Jefferson (1743–1826), for example, the noted American deist, deleted all accounts of miracles when he edited a special version of the New Testament.[11] If, as Jefferson believed, grace and miracles do not exist, then prayer and sacraments, likewise, are meaningless, superstitious rituals. In a similar way the English deist Matthew Tindal (1655–1733) sneered at the "superstitions" of the sacraments. In his *Christianity as Old as the Creation,* Tindal gibed, "What right has a Papist who rubs a dying man with oil to laugh at the Indian who thinks it will conduce to his future happiness to die with a cow's tail in his hands?"[12] Peter Gay, a leading modern scholar on the Enlightenment, sums up the attitude of the English philosopher David Hume (1711–1776), whose world was governed by a remote, impersonal God, in the following words: "Since God is silent, man is his own master: he must live in a disenchanted world, submit everything to criticism, and make his own way."[13]

For Carroll, in contrast, God is not just a far-off, long-ago power and principle of the creation of the universe. God is ". . . the Father of mercies & forgiveness" and is involved lovingly and intimately with the individual person and the affairs of mankind. (pp. 410, 451, 460) He readily offers assistance to those who implore it in prayer. (p. 401) Prayer is the principal means to be used to grow in sanctification through the power of the Holy Ghost. (p. 417) The best means, Carroll testified, through which grace is conveyed, are the sacraments:

> The most effectual means, established by a beneficent providence, the most abundant channels, through which grace may be conveyed to our souls, and we enriched by the merits of Christ's sacred blood, are the Sacraments. (p. 421)

Sacraments are effective because of their divine origin and sanction. The Eucharist is "the great Sacrament of love" as well as ". . . the body & blood of our divine Redeemer." (p. 407) God himself comes to us through the Eucharist: "The food is itself divine, and he, who gives it, is God himself." (p. 407) Penance brings merciful forgiveness and restores our friendship with God. (p. 451) Through Baptism, we receive the gift of faith and through Confirmation we receive the Holy Ghost, which makes us strong, perfect Christians. (pp. 418, 422)

Through his Holy Spirit, the loving God entreats a person inwardly. He speaks to a person's heart, reminding individuals of the danger of hardening their hearts against his calling. (p. 451) Carroll exclaimed,

> Thus it is, O Father of mercies, O God of all consolation, that thou art ever giving proofs of thy goodness towards mankind. More watchful than we ourselves, over our most important concerns, and more affected with our misery, thy providence ceases not to shower down on us undeserved and even unrequested benedictions. Thy bounty feeds us: Thy munificence cloths us; to say nothing of thy liberality in bestowing blessings

of a superior order in anticipating our requests by thy grace, when we become insensible of our duty; and recalling us from the ways, which lead to misery, even when we wilfully forget thy holy law and our own obligations. (p. 438)

God, our father, is more loving and more watchful than we are for ourselves. He provides for our needs in advance and repeatedly calls us back in spite of our willful disobedience. Through the means of religion, the loving God is working for man's lasting happiness with him.[14] His loving providence over human affairs, therefore, can be detected from the continual preservation of religion through his revelation:

. . . they, who attribute nothing in the affairs of mankind to the government of providence, will only discover the result of human counsels and passions; but they, whose enlightened faith beholds in the history of mankind the traces of a divine and overruling wisdom, will acknowledge the power of God continually exerted for the preservation of religion. (p. 460)

The personal God's loving providence operates not only within each individual, but within all the affairs of mankind as well. Thus did Carroll in his thought and preaching oppose the tenets and beliefs of the Enlightenment proponents.

III. PERFECTIBILITY OF MAN AND SOCIETY

Many Enlightenment thinkers were optimistic about the capacity of man's mind and the capability of his will to achieve perfection. Matthew Tindal (1655–1733), for example, claimed that universal truth is evident to all men of reason. God has created rational creatures so that they might, through their own intellectual capacity, know the basic law and will of Divine Reason.[15] Tindall stated in *Christianity as Old as the Creation:*

> Whoever so regulates his natural appetites as will conduce most to the exercise of his reason, the health of his body and the pleasures of his senses taken and considered together may be certain he can never offend his Maker; who, as he governs all things according to their natures, can't but expect his rational creatures should act according to their natures.[16]

Virtue, accordingly, lay in the beliefs and practices of what was most agreeable to men's reason and nature; thus virtue will promote human happiness. Tindal consequently stated his belief that morality could be defined as ". . . acting according to the reason of things considered in themselves."[17] Therefore, it must be assumed that, for Tindal, there was no need for revelation and the interference of God to aid men in their knowledge and practice of virtue. Through their innate moral sense, rational men know what is good and what is evil; through their natural power, rational men can attain perfection. True religion, Tindal continued, consisted ". . . in a constant disposition of mind to do all the good we can, and thereby render ourselves acceptable to God in answering the end of our creation."[18] Tindal thus accentuated man's natural ability to come to the truth of religion by reason, and confidence in his ability to pursue and do good. Man's future rewards lay solely in each individual's performance of those moral duties which his own reason conceived to be the commands of God.

The basis of the *philosophes'* faith in man's power to know the universal law and his ability to act in the light of this knowledge lay in having confidence in his human nature and intellect. Jean Jacques Rousseau (1712–1778) believed in the innate goodness of the innocent, uncorrupted natural man. He extolled the life of the "noble savage" in freedom and goodness. Man was virtuous and happy in his natural state. Civilization had corrupted and enslaved man to egotistic acquisition and inhumanity.[19] Rousseau's conviction of man's natural goodness, then, is irreconcilable with the orthodox Christian understanding of man's inherent fallen condition caused by original sin. When asked about the divinity of Christ later in his life, Benjamin Franklin (1706–1790) responded, "It is a question I do not dogmatize upon, having never studied it, and think it needless to busy myself with it now, when I expect so soon an opportunity of knowing the truth with less trouble."[20]

Many *philosophes* believed that the foundation of man's true liberty lay in autonomy of intellect and will. Authority comes from a rational conviction in men's inherent ability, not from external sources. The solution of autonomy, Kant remarked, lay in man's courage to use his own reason and his own will to follow the conclusion of that reason:

Laziness and cowardice explain why so many men . . . remain under a life-long tutelage and why it is so easy for some men to set themselves up as the guardians of all the rest. . . . Do we now live in an enlightened age? No; but we live in an age of enlightenment. Though certainly much is lacking, the obstacles to the general enlightenment are gradually being reduced. Men are releasing themselves from self-imposed tutelage and learning to deal freely with religious and other matters. . . . As the use of reason gradually spreads and develops it will first have an effect on the character so that men become more capable of managing their freedom.[21]

For the Enlightenment *philosophes,* when man became truly free in this way, his future and that of society would be bright and lead to limitless progress. Man would be able to solve his moral and social problems through the operation of his autonomous rational intellect and rational will. Rational will was capable of acting according to the universal law of reason. God, who created an orderly universe, left it strictly alone. Now it was man's sacred duty to shed the light of reason into the darkness of superstition and deceit, thus bringing enlightenment and the happiness of perfection.

Jean Condorcet (1743–1794), a French contemporary of Kant, expressed his belief in unlimited human progress thus:

> How consoling for the philosopher . . . is this view of the human race, emancipated from its shackles, released from the empire of fate and from that of the enemies of its progress, advancing with a firm and sure step along the path of truth, virtue and happiness.[22]

The perfection of man and society were to be ushered in by the forces of man's reason, new technology and medicine:

> The time will therefore come when the sun will shine only on free men who know no other master but their reason . . . new instruments, machines and looms can add to man's strength . . . preventive medicine improves and food and housing become healthier . . . Would it be absurd then to suppose that this perfection of the human species might be capable of indefinite progress.[23]

Like many other Enlightenment thinkers, Condorcet believed in the perfectibility of man and society on this earth alone achieved solely by human endeavor.

What were Carroll's views on the *philosophes'* optimistic faith in man's nature and reason? Unlike the *philosophes,* Carroll believed that the perfection man was meant to achieve belonged to a higher order. "Christian virtue must be established on the foundation of faith . . ." (p. 417) which consists ". . . not only of obedience of the will to execute the commands of God; but likewise of submission of the understanding to the belief & open acknowledgement of the doctrines revealed by infallible Truth." (p. 386) Carroll stated:

> The just man lives by faith that is, he is preserved in the grace and favor of God, because he knows and embraces those great truths, which animate and support us in the exercise of Christian virtues and necessary self-government. (p. 393)

For Carroll, not only is man's faith continually preserved by God's grace, but his knowledge of the truth also comes from it. With the coming of Holy Ghost, ". . . the light of faith dispelled the darkness, which till then overshadowed their [men's] understandings." Then they "better comprehended" the meaning of the words of God. (p. 408) Hence, in order to know the object of faith and continue in the life of faith, a person needs to submit totally his "understanding to the belief" (386) and to acknowledge "continual dependence on God." (p. 393) Faith, Carroll asserted, which is the foundation of a person's sanctification should be "reared and increased by prayer." Faith grows and perseveres by the power of the Holy Ghost and prayer is the principal means to be employed to this end. (p. 417)

Man needs God's grace because of the limitations of his fallen nature. As Carroll expounded:

The evil . . . is that hereditary evil derived from the prevarication of our first Father; that fatal stain inherent in our nature, which makes us to be conceived in sin, & born children in wrath. (p. 403)

The darkened human mind and corrupted will need divine assistance to know the truth and to will the good:

Let us beseech the Holy Spirit of truth and sanctification . . . to illustrate our minds with the knowledge of the best means of living faithfully attached to the Service of our Creator and to inflame our hearts with ardor to pursue those means. (p. 401)

The gift of grace results from the death of Christ, the Son of God, who offered himself for the sins of humanity:

The Son of God, Priest forever of a much higher order than Aaron and destined to introduce a far more perfect dispensation of grace and religion, comes down from heaven, and by the wonderful and omnipotent operation of the Holy Ghost, assumes and is united to a body, formed of the same materials, as our own. . . . after fulfilling the functions of a Pastor, and prophet, and Legislator, he concludes his life in the office and exercises of a pontiff and victim: for our iniquities, he is covered with his own sacred blood. (p. 405)

Hence, the salvation of human beings, who were enslaved by sin, was realized by

. . . the Son of God offering up his body inseparably united with his Divinity; & presenting his blood &c, exhibits a victim of infinite value &c. The number or enormity of sins cannot equal the merit of such a dignified satisfaction. (p. 406)

Mankind is redeemed because of Jesus' suffering and death. Carroll emphasized the divinity of Christ by equating the word of God with the word of Christ. The Bible is divine revelation and ". . . humbly believing the doctrines of J. C." is a necessity. (p. 388)

Our loving Savior invites us to imitate him in the practice of virtue. (p. 405) To be a disciple of Christ means to follow him in his loving spirit:

> . . . the true spirit and character of Christianity is a spirit of charity and compassion, that it is an illusion to deem ourselves, the Disciples of Christ, without becoming interested in the necessities of our neighbour, and exacting endeavours to relieve them. (p. 437)

The summit of Christian perfection is the love of God (p. 417). Love of God is to love the Lord, one's God, with one's whole heart and mind. This love is expressed in serving God to advance his glory and working for the salvation of oneself and one's neighbors (p. 461), while attending to their corporal needs as well. (p. 436) This love of God and love of neighbor will take us to everlasting happiness where we will testify to "the mercy of our Lord Jesus Christ unto life everlasting." Carroll proclaimed:

> Christian virtue must be established on the foundation of faith; must be reared and increased by prayer; must be completed by the love of God; and rewarded with mercy in life everlasting. (p. 417)

Therefore, Christian perfection and heavenly happiness are due to the fruit of Jesus Christ's suffering and death for sinful humanity. Grace enlightens and preserves faith; grace carries one to the summit of perfection, and grace brings everlasting happiness. In this way Carroll reaffirmed Christian orthodoxy's view of mankind in contradistinction to the Enlightenment thinkers' confidence in unaided human reason and their effort to achieve perfection.

IV. UNIVERSAL RELIGION AND ANTI-CHRISTIANITY

Many thinkers of the Enlightenment believed in the existence of a single universal religion knowable to all rational men. John Toland (1670–1722), yet another English deist, maintained that true religion is accessible to the natural reason of all men and thus absolutely universal.[24] Many American leaders were more or less deists at the time of the struggle for American Independence. Thomas Jefferson (1743–1826), for example, declared: "He who steadily observes those moral precepts in which all religious concur, will never be questioned at the gates of heaven, as to the dogmas in which they all differ."[25] Universal morality, hence, common to all religions, is affirmed while the specifically Christian doctrine is ignored.

Earlier, the German *philosophe* Gotthold Lessing (1729–1781) saw the essence of religion as a humanitarian morality independent of all historical revelations. Lessing believed that no single religion had the whole truth and condemned those who subscribed to a particular system of dogma. All authentic religions, according to Lessing, possess something of the truth, and each religion has something to contribute to the edification of mankind. Believers of all denominations, such as Christians, Jews, and Moslems, were to serve God and their fellows according to the tenets of their respective religious institutions.[26] Lessing encouraged toleration and respect for other religions while each individual followed his own religious traditions. Lessing saw all religions as having educational value for the human race. In Lessing's view, the teachings of Jesus had to be judged by the norms of humanitarian ethics.

All the Enlightenment thinkers emphasized ethical behavior more than doctrine. Many believed that Christianity is merely one religious association among many others, and that its principle function was to foster morality in the same way that other religions do. Anything in religion, Tindal contended, that is not conducive to man's morality should be denounced. The more man ". . . is taken up with the observation of things which are not of a moral nature, the less he will be able to attend those that are."[27] The goal of religion, therefore, was understood to be morality.

Even though the *philosophes* were concerned with religious toleration, they abhorred the dogmatism and intolerance which, for them, characterized organized religion. For Voltaire, organized Christianity was invented by crafty rascals to manipulate untaught masses. He ruthlessly attacked the tyranny of Christianity in tormenting and burning rational men who dared to dispute its dogmas. Voltaire conceived Utopia as a place where peace and freedom could reign without the interference of monks, priests, and without the acrimony of lawsuits. There, people could freely worship God as their reason dictated, and could solve their problems by the use of logic and the advances science would make as a result of the loosening of the "bonds" of the intellect.[28]

Hume deplored that beyond the world of Enlightenment in which he and civilized supporters of it lived, lay a vast realm of ". . . stupidity, Christianity and ignorance."[29] In his analysis of Rome's decline and fall, Edward Gibbon (1737–1794) attributed the cause of the empire's downfall to Christianity. He saw Rome's fall as a triumph of barbarism and religion.[30] For Gibbon, therefore, the spiritual inner cancer of ". . . religion was as barbarizing an influence as the barbarians. . . ." who invaded from without.[31]

Condorcet envisioned a bright future when reason would be the only master of free men and when there would be no tyranny and superstition of Christianity. He expressed his optimistic belief in a future in these words:

. . . priests and their stupid or hypocritical instruments will exist only in works of history and on the stage; and we shall think of them only . . . to learn how to recognize and so to destroy, by force of reason, the first seeds of tyranny and superstition, should they ever dare to reappear amongst us.[32]

In *The Enlightenment: The Rise of Modern Paganism,* Peter Gay sums up the anti-Christian attitude of the *philosophes:*

. . . Christianity claimed to bring light, hope, and truth, but its central myth was incredible, its dogma a conflation of rustic superstitions, its sacred book an incoherent collection of primitive tales, its church a cohort of servile fanatics as long as they were out of power and of despotic fanatics once they had seized control. With its triumph in the fourth century, Christianity secured the victory of infantile credulity; one by one, the lamps of learning were put out, and for centuries darkness covered the earth.[33]

For the *philosophes,* the age of Christianity was an age of superstition, credulity, priestcraft, and persecution. Therefore, they struggled for emancipation from the restraint of Christian dogma and vehemently attacked the Christian institution and its authority.

What was Carroll's opinion of universal religion, recognizable only by reason and of the anti-Christian stand of the *philosophes?* According to Carroll, those who claimed to know everything by natural instinct and reason are enemies of religion. These enemies Carroll charged, pretend

. . . that we know everything by the exercise alone of those natural faculties and that portion of reason, which are granted to every man; that by employing these, we may learn the few principles, to which they reduce all religion, and which, therefore, is called *natural religion* . . . For while they extol the merit and dignity of natural religion, their zeal and malicious purpose is, to inculcate a persuasion that any other manifestation of God's being and providence, any other injunctions of his will, are useless and unnecessary, consequently that there is no revealed religion, and that all pretentions to it are false and interested impositions. (p. 377)

Carroll contended that "the doctrine of men" is of an inferior order to the "doctrine of God" and deserves the condemnation of God:

The insolence of self confidence is strongly reprobated, by which human pride brings the truth of heaven before the tribunal of its own feeble reason, & presumes to judge the wisdom of God, so that the devil cometh & taketh the word out of their heart, lest believing they should be saved. (p. 395)

For Carroll, religion is established on the foundation of God's revelation. The authority of Christianity does not lie within the rational light of human reason; rather it comes from a holy and true God: "Religion derives from its Divine Author, truth & holiness: truth in doctrine, & holiness in its preceptial morality."[34] Carroll asserted that Christianity is superior to a natural religion based on feeble reason, because Christianity is founded ". . . originally from our entire dependence on God, as our 1st beginning and last end."[35] A true and holy God is the author of Christianity, whose true head and founder is Jesus Christ. (p. 460) Hence, Christianity is the true religion and every Christian must honor his religion by ". . . subjecting his understanding to its doctrines.''[36] According to Carroll, not only Christian doctrines, but Church authority, too, has divine authorship. Christ had ordained the priesthood for the perpetuation of his own sacred priesthood according to the order of Melchisedeck. Priests are to teach, offer sacrifice, and reclaim those in sin. (p. 413) Christians are to submit to Church authority which Christ established in his Church. (p. 412)

Carroll addressed those who had full confidence in their natural reason alone in matters of truth and who denied revealed religion in this way:

We cannot open the gospel, without finding in every page the sentence of reprobation pronounced by our blessed Lord against the world. Its doctrines and maxims are placed continually in opposition to those of eternal wisdom and holiness: its conduct is represented as subversive of that worship of God in spirit and truth, which is essential to real religion. (p. 450)

Christianity is not one religious association among many others. Christianity has the revelation of God: without revelation, one cannot come to the essence of a "real religion", i. e., "worship of God in spirit and truth." Worship of God in spirit can be known when one's heart is firmly devoted to God, the Father, and consequently willing to suffer for his will and his law. (p. 401). God would not ". . . accept a worship in which the heart has no share."[37] Such charity is realized by the Holy Spirit. (p. 401) The Church encourages prayer as the principal contact with the Holy Spirit (p. 417), and dispenses sacraments as the effective means of garnering the Holy Spirit. (p. 421) Another aspect of the essence of real religion is to worship God in truth. Christianity is holy and true because its author is the true and holy God. Christianity possesses truth through the revelation of God. Hence, a Christian knows the meaningful obligations of honoring God and serving him by serving fellow creatures. (p. 377) Christianity enables one to worship God "in spirit and truth" which is essential in a true religion. Therefore, Carroll exhorts, the Christian must honor religion.

> As we are of honoring Alm: God: for God is our last end, to which we are obliged to refer our lives & actions; & Religion is the means which connects and unites us with our end; as it is therefore impossible to arrive at the end without embracing the means of coming to it; so it is impossible to honour God without honouring Religion.[38]

God is our end whom we cannot reach without religion. The essence of religion is to honor God which can be done only through ". . . the means of Religion."[39] Christianity, Carroll insists, in rejecting Enlightenment trends, is the unique and true religion because it reveals and assists man in knowing how to honor God "in spirit and truth" through its revealed doctrines—through its teaching and dispensation of sacraments by Church authority.

CONCLUSION

The differences between the key concepts of the Enlightenment and those which Carroll taught are clearly distinguishable. First, the *philosophes* affirmed their faith in human reason alone which would prove the existence of God and necessary norms of morality. Since reason was for them the only genuine guide to truth, the acceptance of truth on another's direction was distasteful and restrictive to the autonomy of reason.

Carroll, on the other hand, emphasized the insufficiency of human reason alone to know the truth. He did not scorn reason, but maintained that only Divine Revelation perfects that which is lacking in the natural power of reason. Only through Revelation does a person know for certain the necessary truth and morality, and, thus gain sufficient motivation to pursue the truth consistently. For Carroll, the Gospel is the word of God, Divine Revelation. It should be, therefore, received with total submission.

Second, the *philosophes* believed in a supreme being who created the universe and ordained the immutable natural laws that govern it. The universe, according to them, was not subject to divine interference. Man had to live according to reason alone, subject everything to its dictates. The concepts of grace, prayer, and sacraments, therefore, were rejected as meaningless superstition.

Carroll, however, maintained that God is a loving Father who is intimately involved in the affairs of the individual and of society. His loving providence aims at the eternal happiness of man. Mankind achieves its goals through God's grace, especially as received in prayer and through the sacraments.

Third, the *philosophes* asserted the possibility of the infinite perfectibility of man and society on the grounds of the goodness of human nature and the autonomy of the human intellect. There was, for them, no need for a redeemer of man. For them, Christ was merely the founder of one religion among many. Christ's teachings, they claimed, need to be judged by the norms of reason and natural-rational morality.

For Carroll, on the other hand, because of original sin, man is inherently deprived of the grace to know and will the good. Christ, the Son of God, redeemed sinful humanity through his suffering and death. Now, perfectibility of man is possible through the fruit of Divine suffering and death, i. e., grace. Christian virtue is the spirit of charity which is the spirit of Christ. Christian virtue is realized in loving God and loving one's neighbors with one's whole being.

Man should submit his understanding to the teaching of Christ because of his Divine authority which reveals it.

Fourth, the *philosophes* affirmed the existence of a universal religion with common morality conceived by all rational people. Religion nurtured morality and the goal of religion was supposed to be morality. For the *philosophes,* religion was an anthropocentric, that is, it was the moral activity of man to achieve the state of morality through natural reasoning. Although the *philosophes* affirmed the idea of universal religion and, thus, encouraged tolerance for other religions, they detested and viciously attacked Christianity. Christianity, they were convinced, represented the enemy of all their "enlightened" thoughts; Christianity prohibited the "Enlightened Age" by its superstition, priestcraft, and tyranny. In opposition to the *philosophes,* Christianity, Carroll insisted, is not one religion among many others: it is the unique and true religion because it was founded on Divine revelation, and the authority of God who is truth and holiness. God is our end and the essence of religion is worshipping God. A person cannot reach God without the divinely revealed religion. For Carroll, religion is theocentric, that is, directed towards the worship of God.

As we have observed, there is a fundamental difference between the concepts and attitudes of the *philosophes* and those of John Carroll. The *philosophes* had an infinite confidence in reason and were totally guided by it. Carroll had an infinite confidence in the wisdom of a loving God and made a total submission to it. There is an irreconcilable opposition between the pragmatic secularism of the *philosophes* and the unconditional faith of Carroll. Close examination of Carroll's sermons reveals that even though Carroll was very much aware of the trends of Enlightenment thought of his day, and familiar with the writings and thoughts of the *philosophes,* he was not affected by them in his piety, in his teaching, or in his exhortations. Carroll remained an enlightened man of faith, but he was not a man of the Enlightenment.

Notes

1. Data about the life of Carroll is drawn from the following sources: Annabelle M. Melville, *John Carroll of Baltimore,* (New York: Charles Scribner's Sons, 1955); Joseph T. Durkin, "The Mission and the New Nation," in *The Maryland Jesuits, 1634– 1833,* R. Emmett Curran, et al. (Baltimore: The Corporation of Roman Catholic Clergymen, 1976), pp. 29–44.

2. Interested readers may consult Joseph P. Chinnici, *Living Stones,* (New York: Macmillan Publishing Company, 1989), pp. 1–34; and Robert Emmett Curran, *American Jesuit Spirituality: The Maryland Tradition, 1634–1900* (Baltimore: The Corporation of Roman Catholic Clergymen, 1976), pp. 1–20.

3. The sermons for the present study are taken mainly from *The John Carroll Papers,* vol. 3, *1807–1815* (Notre Dame: University of Notre Dame Press, 1976), edited by Thomas O'Brien Hanley, except "Confess Our Religion Exteriorly" in *American Jesuit Spirituality: The Maryland Tradition, 1634–1900*. The sermons are not dated; however, the introduction to Hanley's work (p. liii) indicates that a majority of them were written in the period following Carroll's episcopal consecration in 1790.

4. Jerald R. Cragg, *The Church and the Age of Reason 1688– 1789* (New York: Penguin Books, 1970), pp. 75–77; W. T. Jones, *A History of Western Philosophy,* Vol. III, *Hobbes to Hume* (New York: Harcourt Brace Jovanovich, Inc., 1969) pp. 263–264.

5. Isaac Newton, *A Short Scheme of the True Religion,* in *Theological manuscripts* (Liverpool: Liverpool University Press, 1950), p. 52, quoted in William C. Placher, *A History of Christian Theology: An Introduction* (Philadelphia: The Westminster Press, 1983), p. 239.

6. Peter Gay, *The Enlightenment: An Interpretation. The Rise of Modern Paganism* (New York: W. W. Norton and Co., 1966), p. 122.

7. John Dillenberger and Claude Welch, *Protestant Christianity: Interpreted through its Development* (New York: Charles Scribner's Sons, 1954), p. 147.

8. W. T. Jones, *A History of Western Philosophy,* Vol. IV,

Kant and the Nineteenth Century (New York: Harcourt Brace Jovanovich, Publishers, 1975), pp. 7–8.

9. The page numbers appearing in the text refer to the sermons of Carroll in *The John Carroll Papers,* Volume 3, *1807–1815,* edited by Thomas O'Brien Hanley.

10. Cragg, op. cit., pp. 73–74.

11. Placher, p. 261.

12. James C. Livingston, *Modern Christian Thought: From the Enlightenment to Vatican II* (New York: Macmillan Publishing Co., 1971), p. 23.

13. Gay, op. cit., p. 419.

14. Robert Emmett Curran, *American Jesuit Spirituality: The Maryland Tradition, 1634–1900* (New York: Paulist Press, 1987), p. 133.

15. Cragg, op. cit., pp. 159–163.

16. Livingston, op. cit., p. 23.

17. Ibid.

18. Ibid.

19. Cragg, op. cit., p. 238.

20. Benjamin Franklin, Letter to Ezra Stiles, March 9, 1790, in *Autobiography, Poor Richard, Letters* (D. Appleton, 1900), pp. 394–395, quoted in Placher, p. 261.

21. Immanuel Kant, *What is Enlightenment?,* quoted in Jones, *Kant,* p. 8.

22. Jean Condorcet, *Sketch for a Historical Picture of the Progress of the Human Mind,* quoted in Jones, *Kant,* p. 3.

23. Ibid., pp. 2–3.

24. Cragg, op. cit., p. 78.

25. Thomas Jefferson, Letters to Mr. William Canby, Sept. 18, 1813, in *The Writings of Thomas Jefferson,* Vol. 6 (Taylor & Maury, 1854), p. 210, quoted in Placher, op. cit., p. 261.

26. Cragg, op. cit., pp. 249–250.

27. Tindal, *Christianity,* quoted in Livingston, op. cit., p. 23.

28. Gay, op. cit., pp. 168–171; Livingston, op. cit., pp. 27–29.

29. Hume to Hugh Blair and others, April 6, 1765, in *Letters,* I, P. 498, quoted in Gay, op. cit., p. 20.

30. Edward Gibbon, *Decline and Fall of the Roman Empire* quoted in Jones, *Kant,* pp. 4–5.

31. Gay, op. cit., p. 215.

32. Condorcet, *Historical Picture,* quoted in Jones, *Kant,* p. 2.32.

33. Gay, op. cit., pp. 207–208.

34. Curran, *American Jesuit Spirituality,* p. 133.

35. Ibid.

36. Ibid., p. 134.

37. Ibid., p. 133.

38. Ibid.

39. Ibid.

Appendix: Anglo-American Catholic Sermons

The following seven representative sermons and one sermon fragment, on the Eucharist, ecclesiology, and Mary and the saints, are included in this collection through the courtesy of the Special Collections Division of Georgetown University Library where they form part of the American Catholic Sermon Collection. This collection consists of 456 autograph manuscript sermons, two contemporary written transcriptions, and four printed items by forty-four preachers from eighteenth-century Anglo-America. The sermons were culled from the archives of Woodstock College, the Maryland Jesuit Province, and Georgetown University.

In reproducing these sermons here, the editors have made only minimal modifications in the text. The physical format has been preserved as closely as possible, except that marginalia (particularly Mosley's Scriptural citations) have been incorporated in the text. Peculiarities of spelling have been retained, while punctuation and capitalization have been modernized. Italics and quotation marks have been used in place of underlining. Abbreviations have been routinely expanded. The sermons appear in their final form; words, phrases, and, in the case of Bolton's 1772 Assumption sermon, an entire paragraph, which were crossed out in the text, have been deleted.

The following sources have been consulted for biographical information on the preachers: Henry Foley, *Records of the English Province of the Society of Jesus,* Vol. VII (London: Burns and Oates, 1882); William P. Treacy, *Old Catholic Maryland and Its Early Jesuit Missionaries* (Swedesboro, NJ: St. Joseph's, 1889); and Leo Gregory Fink, *Old Jesuit Trails in Penn's Forest* (New York: Paulist Press, 1936).

The authors are grateful to George M. Barringer, head of the Special Collections Division of Georgetown University Library, and to his staff, for permission to publish the sermons here, and for many courtesies extended during the past year.

JOSEPH MOSLEY
Vigilance in the Faith
1758

*Joseph Mosley was born in Lincolnshire, England in
November, 1730 or 1731. He studied at St. Omer's
College in Flanders and was admitted to the Society
of Jesus on September 7, 1748. His older brother,
Michael, had already been a Jesuit for nine years.
Although various sources have him arriving in Amer-
ica in 1759 or 1764, the citation of this sermon, at
McConchie's (a sub-station of St. Thomas Manor in
Charles County) on the Sixth Sunday after Epiphany
in 1758 would appear to place Mosley in Maryland
early in that year. In August, 1764 he went with Father
John Lewis to Bohemia on Maryland's upper Eastern
Shore, and later that month began mission work in
Queen Annes and Talbot Counties. On March 18, 1765
he went with eight black servants and founded St.
Joseph's in Talbot County (present Cordova) and spent
the rest of his life at this lonely outpost as the sole
missionary on the lower Eastern Shore. From his faithfully maintained sacramental registers, and from his
correspondence with his sister in England, we get a
somewhat detailed account of his extensive ministry in
the area. Mosely died on June 3, 1787 and was buried
in the chapel he had erected at St. Joseph's.*

*In this sermon Mosley makes frequent use of Scrip-
ture to urge his congregation to stand fast in their
Catholic faith in the midst of the trials of the world,
particularly their inability to participate in public life.*

McConchies 1758
*Ad Majorem Dei, Deiparo, Sancti Francisci Xaverii Glo-
riam.*
A Sermon for the 6th Sunday after the Epiphany.

*Vos imitatores nostri facti estis, et Domini excipientes
verbum in tribulatione multa, cum gaudio Spiritus Sancti.*
"You became followers of us and of Our Lord; receiving
the word in much tribulation, with joy of the Holy Ghost."
Words taken out of the 1st Epistle of St. Paul to the
Thessalonians, chapter 1, verse 6 and read in the epistle of
the present Sunday.

The great apostle St. Paul, dearest Christians, thought it
a part of his duty and obligation, consequently to admonish
the faithful to be always on their guard, and beware of the
enemies of Jesus Christ, who might be apt frequently either
by powers of words or violence of torments to seduce them.
Yes, in almost every one of his epistles to the neophytes he
encourages them to fight valiantly the battles of the Lord,
to stand steadily against the enemies of the Church, and
firmly to maintain the word of God in whatsoever tribulations and persecutions. *Excipientes verbum in tribulatione
multa.* (I Thessalonians 1: 6). He frequently exhorts them,
he instructs them how to behave in their necessities, he
proposes to them the example of Jesus Christ, of his fellow
laborers, and of himself. The reason why this apostle used
such vigilance is very plain and obvious, for he has his
flock daily opprest, many seduced by reason of their insupportable sufferings from the enemies of Jesus Christ. He
saw the gospel contemn'd and calumniated, he saw religion
laught at, and devotions contemn'd as nothing but hypoc-
risy. And it is the same reason, dearest Christians, that
induces me to think it my indispensable obligation to encourage you to bear firmly and steadily all calumnies and
persecutions, that are raised in our heretical country by
our inveterate enemy, and lay before your eyes the rewards

Christ has promised those that persevere faithful to the end. For I see you no less opprest than the flock of St. Paul, and your enemies not less numerous. I see the devout and pious scoft at, the gospel trampelled under foot and the Church slited and abused. Wherefore in this my discourse, I propose in my 1st point to show that it is the will of God you should be so opprest either to show his particular love toward you, or to try your fidelity, or in fine to satisfy for sins, with which you offend his infinite goodness. In my 2nd point I'll encourage you by laying before you the great glory and reward Christ has prepared for his partners in his sufferings. I beg your favourable attention.

1st Point

There is no one I believe, that sees how our unfortunate and unhappy country lies wallowing in the mire of heresy and sin, how it is plunged into error and darkness, filled with enemies of the Catholick Church, and sworn persecutors of those who profess that holy name, that does not at the same time perceive that of consequence those who profess this Catholick religion must be opprest, persecuted, calumniated, injured, and heavier burdens laid on them than on the rest of the nation, and since it is possible that some under these heavy burdens may grieve and repine, and accuse the divine goodness of cruelty and tyranny, let them understand that they are seduced and led into an error and do not as yet comprehend the maxims and principles of the gospel.

I confess we lie under heavy burdens and almost insupportable inconveniences, yet at the same time I know, that they are the gift of God both to try our constancy and fidelity in his service, and more plentifully to reward us afterwards. Yes, dearest Christians, these are marks of his love and affection towards us, for he says himself, *quos amo, arguo et castigo.* (Apocalypse 3:19). "Whom I love, I reprehend and chastise." Now, dearest Christians, who can complain God is to hard on him, if he hears from his divine goodness those comfortable words that ought to enliven our spirits against whatsoever adversity, *quos amo, arguo et castigo*; "whom I love, I reprehend and chastise." Behold then, dearest Christians, you are objects of God's love. Rejoice rather than repine, for you are happy as Christ says, if the world hates and persecutes you. *Beati estis qui maledixerint vos homines, et persecuti vos fuerint, et dixerint omne malum adversum vos mentientes, propter me.* (Matthew 5:11). Nay even, dearest Christians, persecutions are such an evident sign of his love, that he did not exempt his own beloved Son from being injured, hated and laughed at. *Ego autem sum vermis,* says he of himself, *et non homo; opprobrium hominen, et abjectio plebis.* (Psalms 21:7). "I am a worm, and not a man, the shame of men and the outcast of the people." Yes, dearest Christians, the greatest blessing this dying God could leave his dear apostles was no other than promising them they should be hated by the whole world. *Eritis odio omnibus propter nomen meum.* (Luke 21:17). "You shall be hated by all for my name." And he says again, *Trademini parentibus et fratribus, et cognatis, et amicis, et morte afficient ex vobis.* (Luke 21:16). "You shall be delivered up to death by your parents, and brothers, and relatives and friends."

Now, dearest Christians, since all the world knows your afflictions hardly to be inferior of those of the apostles, we must confess of consequence that you are not less beloved. O good God, what a happiness, what a benefit! Who amongst you does not willingly cry out with St. Augustin, *Hic fume, hic sera, hic ne parcas, ut in aeternum parcas.* "Here burn me, here torture me, here show me not the least mercy, that you may have mercy on me forever hereafter."

But, dearest Christians, his love is not the only reason why he chastises his elect. It is also to try their fidelity and love. For it is a maxim admitted by all that no one can show more evidently his love, than by suffering for him we love.

This the great St. Gregory meant when he said, *Probatio dilectionis est exhibitio operis,* "The proof of love is the performing of deeds. Yes, dearest Christians, to your unspeakable comfort Christ himself in the gospel has affirmed the same but in stronger terms. *Majorme dilectionem nemo habet, ut animam suam ponat pro amicis suis.* (John 15:13). "No one can show greater love, than by laying down his life for his friends." Now, dearest Christians, If Christ has said that no one can show greater love than by dying for his friend, and since such an occasion of happiness won't in all probability befall any of us in regard of God, I may from those same words bring a lawful consequence, that he that comes the nearest death, will also show the greatest love. And I believe there is no one that has experienced it will deny injuries, affronts, loss of estates, afflictions, tribulations, incapacity of publick offices to approach the nearest death any thing can in this life. Nay, even the loss of honours and a good name is reputed by some to be worse than death itself. You see them, dearest Christians, it is by tribulations that our love is put to the test. It is tryed by them as gold in the glowing furnace, *tamquam aurum in fornace probavit illos.* (Wisdom 3:6). God exposes us to the miseries and calamities of this world to see where we are fit to be companions of his Son, Jesus Christ, and champions that are worthy of himself. *Deus tentavit eos, et invenit eos dignos se.* (Wisdom 3:5). "God tried them and found them worthy of himself." Thus he tempted David, whom he confessed to be a man according to his own heart, as also Abraham, *pater Abraham tentatus est, per multas tribulationes probatus, Dei amicus effectus est.* (Judith 8:22). Thus he tried Job who was reduced to such misery in the eyes of the world all thought God had rejeted him. Yet he bears all with pateince so far as to say, *etiamsi me occiderit, sperabo in eum.* (Job 13:15). In fine to say nothing of other martyrs who so courageously shed their blood in the gospel's cause. I'll only propose to you your own countrymen, who, only in the last century chose rather to be hanged under that bloody standard of the holy martyrs, than suffer themselves to be robbed of the faith in which they so much gloried. We see them hurried to prison, tortured on a rack, accused by false witnesses, draged thro the streets, hanged and quartered. Faith was the cause; love drove them on. It was nothing but divine love that made them fast in these dreadful torments. And could you, dearest Christians, in proof of the same love, undergo the loss of your estates and permit yourselves to be accounted fools for your master, Jesus Christ. He first loved you and for that love he has gone the way of the Cross. He has suffered ignominy, been falsely accused, and condemned in fine to an infamous death. And now he only demands of you, what no one can deny to be his right, love for love.

I can't persuade myself but that you are all now willing to be tried like gold in the furnace. I think I hear you say out with the confidence and resolution of the royal prophet, *Si consistant adversum me castra, non timebit cor meum.* (Psalms 26: 3). I imagine I see no less doubt than was in the breast of St. Thomas the Apostle when he said unto his companions, *Eamus et nos, ut moriamur cum eo.* (John 11:16). Yes, dearest Christians, of what ought we to be afraid? Love drives us on; Christ leads the way. He is at the head of the afflicted. Be now his worthy companions. *Eamus et nos, ut moriamur cum eo.* Account your estates as nothing, value little whether you are hated for Jesus Christ and his gospel. Heaven is your country, your estates are not here. Then *eamus et nos, ut moriamur cum eo.* Stick steadily to your faith, adhere firm to your religion, against whatsoever oppositions, your enemies can only hurt the body, but the soul they can't endanger. *Animam autem non possunt occidere.* (Matthew 10:28).

But yet notwithstanding what I've already said, dearest Christians, some may as yet wonder why God acts with such a cruel and tyranical part. I answer with the Church, *that it is true that* God is infinitely merciful, but yet it is not less true that he is infinitely just. That is, since there are always sinners to be found amongst the just and elect people of God, and since sinners are not to often accustomed to render God due satisfaction, God is free, nay even obliged out of his infinite justice to require it, either in this world, or in the next. So that I think no one can wonder that God acts (to make use of their expressions) such a tyrranous part and chastises them who've had the boldness to offend him. For justice according to the Scripture always demands equal atonement to the crime committed. *Pro mensura peccati erit et plagarum modus.* (Deuteronomy 25:2). Wherefore now I may say to you, what God said to the Jews on another occasion, *Qui sine peccato est vestrum, primus in illam lapidem mittat.* (John 8:7). That is, let him complain in the 1st place, that God is cruel and tyrranical, who can brag he has no sin on his conscience, nor has any way offended the divine majesty, so as to deserve to be punished. But some perchance may say that the just are equally afflicted with the sinner. Tis true; the just share sometimes of the miseries God sends the sinner, because he loves them, as I've said above, and has also a mind to try their love and fidelity. Wherefore in a word, I say, some sinners are permitted here because God intends they shall live with him hereafter. The just are also afflicted to prove their love and fidelity towards God. Other sinners have not that happiness but are left wallowing in their iniquities enjoying all the comfort and pleasure this life can afford them. They live daintily. They seek their ease, pass away this life in joys and delights, but in a minute descend to hell. *Incuit in bonis dies suos et in puncto ad inferna descenderunt.* (Job 21:13). Behold then, dearest Christians, the happiness to suffer in this life; for he that lives happy and at his ease here will find nothing but misery and torments hereafter. Thus the Gospel, *recipisti bona in vita tua, nunc autem hic consolatur.* (Luke 16:25). But on the contrary he that passes this life in misery and afflictions may expect in the next to reign with God for ever. *Hic similiter mala, nunc autem consolatur.* (Luke 16:25). For it does not seem reasonable to expect comfort both in this life, and in the life to come. Choose then, dearest Christians, what wisdom dictates. For my part I would have fulfilled on me the words of Christ, *Zion amo, abjuro et castigo.* That is, if I've a mind to be loved by Christ, I must expect to be chastised by him, for his chastisements proceed justly out of love. For he sees your sin and like a loving father chastises you for it, that you may have an occasion to satisfy his divine goodness in this life which is far from a desire he has to see you afflicted. He intends only to ransom you from the jaws of hell, and the power of the devil. *Flagella Domini,* says the invincible Judith, *quibus quasi servi corripimur ad emendationem et non ad perditionem nostram evenisse credamus.* (Judith 8:27). If the scourge of the Lord overtakes us, we must not think that he sends it for our perdition, but for our emendment. Infine, "you are just, Lord, and your judgments are equitable." *Justus est, Domine, et rectum judicium tuum.* (Psalms 118:137). If wherefore, dearest Christians, if you are only all persuaded, there is no one I believe will dare to complain, but on the contrary cry out to the Almighty. *Sta super me, et interfice me.* (II Kings, 1:9). "Stand over me, Lord, and kill me if it is your will." Or with the acts of conformity which an agonizing God used in the Garden of Gethsemani, *Pater mi, si non potest hic calix transire nisi bibam illum, fiat voluntas tua.* (Matthew 26:42). If I can't, O Lord, pass this life without offending you, and of consequence being lyable to punishment, I beg not to be exempted from them. But rather if it is your will, lett them come. I'll try to sustain them. I'll be faithful to my God, I'll be constant in my religion against all enemies and oppositions my loving Father pleases to send me. *Pater mi!* "for my heart is ready, O Lord! my heart is ready."

Paratum cor meum, Deus, paratum cor meum. (Psalms 107:1). "So let your will be done," *fiat voluntas tua.*

The reward God has promised those that suffer shall now be the subject of my 2nd point.

2nd Point.

But altho, dearest Christians, weighty may be the reasons which I've already alleged to persuade you patiently and valiantly to undergo the afflictions and tribulations you lay under in this unfortunate land; yet an other remains which may be as powerful and efficacious to you as any. This is the secure reward God has promised those that are faithful companions of his Son, Jesus Christ in his afflictions. *Beati qui persecutionem patiuntur,* (Matthew 5:10), says this suffering God himself in the Gospel, *quoniam ipsorum est regnum coelorum.* "Blessed are those that suffer persecution for justice's sake, because their's is the kingdom of heaven." That is to say, that they suffer in the Gospel's cause, that are condemned for Jesus Christ, that are persecuted for God and their religion, are in a happy and secure state, "for theirs is the kingdom of heaven." *Quoniam ipsorum est regnum coelorum,* Yes, heaven is their own. They have purchased it by their labours, they have fought faithfully, they have defeated their enemy, nothing remains but to carry off the crown and enjoy their victories. They may now even cry to the divine goodness with St. Paul, *bonum certamen certavi, de reliquo reposita est mihi corona justitiae, quam reddet mihi Dominus.* (II Timothy 4:7). "I've successfully fought the battle, and what remains, there is a crown of justice prepared for me, which God will render me."

But yet, dearest Christians, it is not precisely for having suffered for Jesus Christ in some part of your life. No, you must persevere unto the end, you must remain firm until it pleases his divine majesty to call you from your labours, to enjoy eternal bliss. For St. Bernard says, "Perseverance is the only vurtue that is crowned;" and our Saviour says also, *qui persevaverit usque ad finem, his salvus erit.* (Matthew 10:22, 24:13). "He that perseveres to the end shall be saved." It is therefore, dearest Christians, by hardships, by labours, by afflictions, by sufferings and these faithfully bore with to the end that you gain the love of God. Nay even our Saviour says these are necessary means. *Regnum coelorum vim patitur.* (Matthew 11:12). "The kingdom of heaven suffers violence." Violence therefore is necessary to enter the gates of heaven, for the way is thro thorns and briars, difficult and hard, and happy those who use proper means to find it. *Quam angusta porta, et arcta via est quae ducit ad vitam et pauci sunt qui inveniunt eam.* (Matthew 7:14). "How narrow is the gate, and straight the road that leads to life, and few there are that find it." And I may lawfully affirm that those are the few that find it that suffer persecutions for justice's sake. This doctrine St. Paul also confirms when he says, *nullus coronabitur nisi legitime certaverit.* (II Timothy 2:5). "No one shall be crowned unless he has fought lawfully." It is therefore by fighting, by the troubles of a hard, laborious and difficult war, you may securely hope to obtain what you so much desire. You are now in the way, only keep your feet firmly, stand your enemy and rather dy than be overcome. Rejoice then, dearest Christians, yours is the crown you've valiantly sought the day. Rejoice, I say, *Gaudete in illa die, et exultate ecce enim merces vestra multa est is coelo.* (Luke 6:23). Your reward is great, says Christ, in heaven it the world hates and persecutes you, and in an other place he not only says it is great but copious, superabundant, as it were overflowing. *Cum maledixerint vobis. Gaudete et exultate quoniam merces vestra copiosa est in coelis.* (Matthew 5:12). Yes, dearest Christians, from these words of Christ I may lawfully infer, that we can't please his divine majesty more by any other virtue, than by that of patience, suffering for the name of

Jesus Christ, for we see our Saviour only reward other virtues with heaven, while for this he not only gives heaven, but also affirms that the reward shall be copious and abounding. *Quoniam merces vestra copiosa est in coelis.* Nay even St. Paul seems to affirm that there is no living piously in Jesus Christ without suffering and persecutions, and of consequence few hopes of eternal bliss. *Omnes qui volunt pie vivere in Christo Jesu, persecutionem patientur* (II Timothy 3:12). And what could Christ our captain else mean when he said, *si quis vult venire post me, et tollat crucem suam.* (Matthew 16: 24). "If any will follow me, let him take up his cross." As if he would say that there was no following him to heaven, but by the way of the cross. That is the way of the cross is necessary to gain heaven, and he that is not willing to be on this way, and yet is loaded with all kinds of virtue, is not in the way to eternal bliss. Good God! if this be true! as certainly it is, thrice happy they, whom God favours with such a blessing and such an evident sign of their happy predestination.

Conclusion

From what has been said, dearest Christians, I can't persuade myself but that you are all convinced, that the way of the cross is a necessary way to heaven. Now then is the time, make a wise choice. If you choose to live at your ease, to escape these troubles, to deny Christ and his holy religion, of consequence you must expect to hear thundered against you those dreadful words, uttered by an angry God, *qui negaverit me coram hominibus, negabo et ego eum coram patre meo.* (Matthew 3:33). "If any one denies me before men, I'll deny him before my father." Take care then, dearest Christians, be cautious; consider well what you are doing. If you deny Christ here in this life, he will deny you before his heavenly Father. But what do I say? Can any one, good God, that is in his senses, make such a choice? No, no! I am certain you will ask, rather cry out, with one of the sons of the invincivle mother, *parati sumus mori magis quam Dei leges praevaricari.* "We are sooner ready to dy, than offend against God's laws." Nay, I don't call in question but that, "neither death nor life, nor angels nor any other creature can separate you from the love of God." *Neque mors, neque vita, neque angeli neque creatura alia poterit nos separare a charitate Dei.* (Romans 8:38). Courage then, dearest Christians, fight on the battle that you are engaged in, for God will reject you if you look back, as unfit for the kingdom of heaven. But if you persist, his grace will be with you. He'll guard you, he'll take care not a hair of your head is touched against his will. It was in this St. Paul confided when he said, *omnia possum in eo, qui me confortat.* (Philippians 4:13). "I can do all things in him, that strengthens me." And if your confidence be like that of the apostle, the grace of God will lead you safe thro all the dangers and storms of this tempestuous sea, and crown you at last with eternal bliss, which God in his infinite goodness grants us all. *In nomine Patris, etc. 1752.*

AUGUSTIN JAMES FRAMBACH
The Holy Eucharist
1762

Augustin James Frambach was born in Germany on January 6, 1729, and entered the Society of Jesus on October 19, 1744. He came to the Maryland Mission together with James Pellentz and two English Jesuits in 1758 and remained there for the rest of his life. Frambach went first to minister to the German Catholics at Conewago, a mission station begun in 1741 in Pennsylvania about fifteen miles north of Gettysburg. In 1769 he began ministering to the Catholics at Frederick in western Maryland, actually living at the station for some ten years before returning to the older mission at Conewago. He left Conewago in 1792, and died at St. Inigoes, Maryland on August 17, 1795.

From the citations it appears that Frambach used this sermon for the Feast of Corpus Christi on several occasions. The earliest date mentioned in 1762 at Pomfret, and later at Cornwallis' Neck both sub-stations of St. Thomas Manor in Charles County. Later he mentions using the sermon at Conewago in 1770, and also cites the home of Mrs. Elder, a prominent Catholic family at Frederick, Maryland.

Conewago
1770
Festo Corporis Christi

"A certain man made a great supper and invited many."
Luke 14: 16.

Exordium: Under the figure of the supper here mentioned in the words of my text, is signified the Sacrament of the Holy Eucharist, which contains the real body and blood of Jesus Christ. And it is indeed a supper truly great, a supper fitter for angels than men! For is it not a banquet of inestimable value? Because God almighty gives us in this heavenly supper his own body and blood for the food and nourishment of our souls, we may therefore with just reason call it a great supper. And yet, how great soever this supper is, the very meanest of us have the honour to be invited to it; nay we are not only invited, but even prayed and importuned to come, and our Saviour is highly displeased if we refuse to come to this heavenly banquet. What infinite goodness is this? What inestimable love of Christ is this, to invite us poor worms of the earth, to invite miserable and ungrateful sinners, to be partakers of the bread of angels; to raise them from the dust, and place them at the table of the king of heaven and earth, to give them the true body and blood of Christ. This real presence of Christ in the Blessed Sacrament we must believe, because we learn it from the express words of truth itself, so often repeated in holy Scripture. We learn it from the express declaration of the Church of God, against which the gates of hell can never prevail. Upon these two pillars of truth, the Word of God, and the Church of God, the faithful Christian securely rests. We must believe, therefore, what the Word of God and the Church of God teaches us. We must believe, that our Saviour Jesus Christ, before his death and passion, has instituted this Blessed Sacrament of the Holy Eucharist. We must believe, that Christ at his Last Supper with his disciples has given to them his true body and blood, and the same body and blood Christ gives us in the Blessed Sacrament. This is an article of faith, because Christ himself has sayd "This is my body and blood." (Matthew 26). Which words are explained by the common opinion of the Catholick Church in a true sense; that Christ has given truly and realy his body and blood to his apostles at the Last Supper, and that Christ gives us daily the same blood and body in the Blessed Sacrament. Therefore, we must captivate our understanding to the obedience of faith; no proud thought of opposition must arrise in us against this great Mystery. We ought to remember, that the merit of faith is to believe what we cannot see; that God almighty can do infinitely more than we can comprehend.

I hope I speak to none here, as to such as are true faithful Christians; as to such as make no difficulty in believing the real presence of Jesus Christ in the Blessed Sacrament. Therefore, my design is not to prove the real presence of Christ in the Blessed Sacrament. The words of Christ are clear enough, and the doctrine of the Church ought to be our rule in believing. I will speak only to day of the great benefit we receive by the Holy Communion, and of the preparation which is necessary for it. The great benefit and the great fruits we receive in the Blessed Sacrament shall be the subject of my first point. The preparation we ought to make before receiving this Blessed Sacrament shall be the subject of my second point, and the whole subject of my present discourse and your favourable attention.

All the sacraments are sacred, and mysterious signs of Divine graces which through them are conveyed to our souls. But the Blessed Sacrament in particular, as it is the greatest of all the the sacraments, contains more and greater mysteries than any of the rest, because in this Blessed Sacrament Jesus Christ gives himself to us under the form of bread. Jesus Christ, says Saint John in his sixth chapter, "is the living bread which came down from heaven, for the life of the world." Therefore the Sacrament of the Eucharist has this advantage above all the other sacraments, that it imparts to the soul the very source of grace, from which all graces flow, by giving us Jesus Christ himself, the author of all graces; by giving us the true body of Christ, his blood, his soul, and his divinity. And therefore it is the most excellent of all the sacraments, and the most plentiful in its fruits. Christ declares it enough in Saint John sixth chapter, where he says *Caro mea vere est cibus, et sanguis meus vere est potus.* "My flesh is meat indeed, and my blood is drink indeed." The proper effect of meat and drink is to preserve life, and consequently it may truly be said to give life to the eaters and drinkers of it. Since, therefore, the flesh and blood of Christ are truly meat and drink, this Divine Sacrament will give life to those that worthily eat and drink at it. This Divine Sacrament, I say, will give a life that is everlasting, according to the expressive words and promises of Christ, saying in Saint John sixth chapter "He that eateth my flesh and drinketh my blood hath life everlasting."—inasmuch as this Divine Sacrament supports our spiritual life by the abundance of graces which it furnishes for the food and nourishment of our souls. It gives us new strength and vigour to carry on happily in our journey towards heaven—"This is the bread that strengthens the heart of man." (Psalm 103)—that gives us force against all temptations, that weakens our passions and concupiscences, that enables us to grow daily in virtue, till we arrive to that everlasting life in heaven.

But this Heavenly Sacrament not only feeds us, nourishes, and strengthens the soul, in order to the maintaining in us the life of grace here, and the bringing us to the life of glory hereafter; but also this Divine Sacrament tends in a particular manner to unite us by a union of love with our God, and transform us in Christ himself. "He that eateth my flesh,'' saith our Lord, John 6th, ''and drinketh my blood, abideth in me, and I in him.'' And is it possible, that he, who abides in Christ, should not abide for ever? Since he abides in him, who abides for ever in the eternal Father. Hence plainly appears, that the food he gives us to eat in his Holy Sacrament, cannot be any temporal food of bread and wine, since this is perishable and cannot therefore produce in its effect, what it had not in itself; *videlicet,* an everlasting existence, and a duration of life without end. The manna, with which God fed the children of Israel for forthy years in the wilderness, was but a figure of that bread of life, which we receive in the Blessed Sacrament: an illustrious figure indeed, but nothing in comparison with the Truth. ''Moses did not give you the bread from heaven,'' says our Lord to the Jews, John 6, for the manna only came down from the clouds, ''but my Father giveth you the true bread from heaven. I am the living bread, which came down from heaven. If any man eat of this bread, he shall live for ever: and the bread that I will give is my flesh for the life of the world. As the living Father hath sent me, and I live by the Father; so he that eateth me, the same also shall live by me. This is the bread, that came down from heaven. Not as your fathers did eat manna, and are dead. He that eateth this bread shall live for ever. He that eateth me, shall live by me,'' says Christ. The corporal food, which we take by the means of our natural heat and digestion, is changed into our corporal substance; but this spiritual food changes us into Christ himself. So that we may say, *Vere vivit in me Christus,* Christ verily lives in me. He that receives worthy Christ in the Sacrament, is incorporated in Christ, he abide in him; and if he is incorporated in Christ, he shall live without danger of every dying, he shall conserve himself without the fear of ending. *Accedat, credat, incorporaetur, ut vivificetur,* says St. Augustin. O sacred bread of life; a wonder, and fruitful Sacrament, which contains an infinite treasure, which contains an inexhaustible source of Divine grace. O Blessed Sacrament! Which contains the living bread, the food, the nourishment, the strength, and the life of our souls; the manna of heaven; the tree of life; the life itself. O Divine Sacrament, which contains the sacred body and blood of Jesus Christ, together with his soul and Divinity; so rich a present, that heaven can give nothing greater! O happy banquet, in which we feed upon the bread of heaven, and drink at the very source of the fountain of life. To this heavenly banquet the Son of God invites all the faithful in the most loving manner: "Come to me," says he, "all you that labour, and are burdened, and I will refresh you." (Matthew 11). Ah! Christians, we all labour, and lie under many and very heavy burthens, from the sins and miseries to which we are exposed during our mortal life, and in this heavenly banquet, we come to Christ to be refreshed, nourished, and strengthened by him. O sweet invitation, O happy call to the source of grace here, and of endless glory hereafter!

But, Dear Christians, if after so sweet an invitation, anyone should refuse to come to this heavenly banquet, if anyone should neglect to correspond to such loving invitation; how much our Lord must be offended by all such, as refuse to come to this divine table! Our Lord has prepared this banquet out of pure love, that we may feast with him, and he with us. He desires, out of pure love, to impart himself, his own sacred body and blood, and all his goods, to us. And therefore he is justly offended, if we should refuse to come to to this Divine Sacrament, if we should prefer the world and its pleasures before him and his banquet. Dear Christians, if you have any love for Christ, surely, you must be desirous of going to him, and entertaining yourselves with him, in this great banquet of love, as to be united in Christ, and to live in him. Christians, if you have any love for yourselves, and for your own souls, you must gladly go to this banquet, in which you find all your good, and all that can make you truly happy, both here and hereafter.

Truth itself assures us, that without this heavenly food, we have no life in us: "Unless you shall eat the flesh of the Son of Man, and shall drink his blood, you shall not have life in you." (John 6: 54). As then we are most strictly bound to maintain the life of our souls, so we are strictly bound to use this food of life in the Most Blessed Sacrament. Because without this heavenly bread we cannot be long preserved from the death of sin, we cannot maintain in us the life of grace. This experience sufficiently teaches, in the primitive times when Christians communicated more frequently, they were more devout, and were enabled by the virtue of this Sacrament not only to keep to whole law of God, but to die martyrs for it. All the saints, that have lived since, did they not communicate frequently? And if we regard the lives of Christians at present, it is plain to be seen, that those who communicate often, are generally the most devout, the most eminent for piety and religion, and most regular in their lives, the most virtuous and the best portion of God's church. While, on the other hand, those who communicate seldom, very seldom, are never the most remarkable for the purity and regularity of their lives. This rule will ever hold. It is vain for any one to plead against frequent Communion. It is in vain to say, they are unworthy, because it is in every one's power to remedy that. It is in every one's power to clear his conscience by a good and sincere confession, and by a hearty contrition, by a sincere and firm resolution to emend their wicked lives, to overcome their sinful habits. Finally, it is in every one's power, to do his best to prepare himself by the help of God's grace for worthy approaching to the table of the Lord. And if you, Dear Christians, with this diligent preparation, would take up a custom of communicating oftener, very likely you would be more worthy every day; whereas the longer you abstain through sloth from this Divine Banquet, the worse you grow. To have no zest, or relish, for the food of life, for Holy Communion, is a certain sign of a disordered conscience, of a brest loaded with the things of this earth, with worldly vanitys; or which is still worse, with sin and sinful passions, with criminal notices and conversations, which they are not as yet resolved to forgoe, and to overcome. And when a person in this unhappy state of inrepetency remains unconcerned, and differs from time to time to partake of this heavenly food, it is an undoubted sign, that he is either dead to God by sin, or will soon die for want of this heavenly food of life.

I call you to witness, Dear Christians; have you ever known one, that worthily frequented this divine table, who was habituated in any vice, or addicted to any sinful habit; and cannot I. And you and all mankind bear witness that those, who communicate but once a year, bear the character of libertines, and men of loose morales. I apeale to those, who have had the care of souls for many years. They tell us in their writings publish'd to the world; they tell us, that of those that approach to Divine Communion but once a year, not one in a thousand lives long in the state of grace. They tell us that our moral life can not be long preserved without food and nourishment; so the grace of God, which is the life of the soul, cannot be long preserved without the bread of life. I convince you, Dear Christians, to bear witness against your selfes: did you ever live well, since you experienced in yourselves that disgust, that unwillingness and backwardness to approach to the divine table? No, no; this unwillingness and disgust proceeded from your bad way of living, and the same unwillingness to receive this Blessed Sacrament, by a mutual causality, enforces, and enlarges daily, your loose way of living. Fewer communions, less grace, less fervour, less spiritual life and vigor—for the proper effect of this Sacrament is to repare our spiritual ruins, to give us new strength against temptations, to give our souls new life and vigour, new graces. Fewer communions, [hence] less zeal for salvation, less regard for spiritual dutys, less watchfulness over their conduct. Those who communicate very seldom commonly forsake all usual acts of piety; they have no regard for sermons, no teast in spiritual things, no devotion in prayer, nor do they call themselves to account by taking into consideration the state of their conscience. And thus being relented in fervour and piety, what is it wonder, that God almighty draws himself and his graces from them. What wonder is it, that their vices grow, their vicious habits take roote, and by consequence they live a loose and sinful life. See, Dear Christians, in what great want we are of this heavenly food, of this Divine Communion. See what benefits, what fruits we receive in this Divine Sacrament. It is true, the transcendent holiness of this Divine Sacrament requires a great purity of soul and conscience, and a great precaution, a great preparation is necessary to communicate well. This necessary preparation before Communion shall make the subject of my second point.

St. Paul, speaking about the necessary preparation before Communion, says: "Let a man prove himself, and so eat of that heavenly bread." (1 Corinthians 11:28). That is, let a man try and examine himself, by looking well into the state of his conscience; let him disburden himself of all sins by an entire confession, and "so eat of that heavenly bread." Lest otherwise approaching to it "unworthy," he make himself "guilty of the body and blood of the Lord," v. 29. So that the first, and most essential, disposition or preparation to a worthy Communion is purity of conscience, at least from all mortal sin. Whosoever presumes to approach to purity itself, in these sacred mysteries, must be clean and pure. *"Sancta Sanctis,"* holy things are for them that are holy. "God will be sanctified in them that approach to him." (Leviticus 10). Who is there, Dear Christians, that does not cleanse his house, and remove whatever is unseemly in it, when he is to receive some noble person for his guest? And is it not more due to God, that a Christian should cleanse his heart, and empty it of all indecency, when he is about to entertain the Divine Majesty; casting out all predominant passions, all carnal, sensual, and worldly appetites, that Christ alone might have the chief command and sovereignty in the heart and soul. What greater incivility, what greater crime can a man be guilty of, than to entertain so great a guest as God himself, amidst a rabble of worldly and sinful affections, and an unruly multitude of carnal appetites, and revengfull passions. God almighty will execute justice justice and judgment on them that defile, and profane his sanctuary, by receiving the holy of holies with a soul polluted with wilful sin, or sinful inclinations. O, Dear Christians, how great is the guilt of a Communion, made without this disposition of purity of conscience. It is a most grievous sacrilege, by profaning the most holy of all the sacraments. It is a most heinous injury and afront ofered to our Lord himself in person, by bringing him into a polluted habitation. A soul under the guilt of mortal sin is possessed by devils: the unworthy communicant, therefore, introduces the Lord of glory into a habitation of unclean spirits. An unworthy communicant imitates the treason of Judas, by betraying his Lord and Master to his enemies. He lays violent hands on our Lord like the Jews; and like them is guilty of the body and blood of Christ. We should have a horror of the wretch, who, by wilful murder, had been guilty of innocent blood. What then ought we to think of ourselves, if, by an unworthy Communion, we should be "guilty of the blood" of the Son of God himself; of that innocent Lamb, immolated for our sins? Would not such a crime as this cry out to heaven for vengeance? Would it not very much darken the understanding, and harden the heart? Would it not put the soul even in the broad road of final inpenitence? It would be, according to the Apostle, receiving judgment, that is, damnation to ourselves. Oh what penance, what flood of tears, would be required to expiate so great a guilt. We have a terrible example of an unworthy communicant in that treacherous disciple Judas. Christ celebrated his Last Supper, and gave his own body and blood to this unworthy disciple; Christ entered also into the breast of Judas, which was harder than a stone, since it was not softned with the blood of the Lamb of God. Scarce had this unworthy communicant, being polluted with an avaritious affection to money, received this divine morsel, but behold, he is punished by being given up unto Satan. *Post buccellam tunc introivit in eum Satanes,* (John 13).) (After the morsel then Satan entered into him.) What presumption is this of the devil? Where Christ enters to lodge himself, does Satan dare to come, and make his abode? St. Ambrose expresses it excellently well in his 12th sermon upon Psalm 118, where he says: Satan came and entered into him, and began to say "He is not thine, O Jesus, but mine; his whole thoughts are taken up in my concern. Thou givest him the bread of heaven, but I have given him money." Which is as much as to say: You, O Lord, are master of him, who receives you worthy in the Sacrament. But he, that still remains a slave of his own affections and sinful appetites, as Judas did to the love of money, cannot have Christ for his Master, and so he abides not in Christ, but in his own sinful affections, which deliver him into the hands of Satan. O unhappy disciple! Unhappy both for time and eternity! Dear Christians, to prevent in us unworthy Communion, let us cleanse our heart from all mortal sin, let us purify it from all affections to a wilful sin.

The second preparation before Communion is a purity of heart, not only from all mortal sin, but from all afections to wilful sin. For God, as he is a jealous lover of the souls of men, will not permit them to place their afections on any other thing, than but himself. For Christ will clame the whole heart of man for himself, without leaving the least place of it empty for any thing, that is not himself, nor aggreable to his Divine Laws. When, therefore, Christ enters within the heart of man, he takes a view of his affections, examines his desires, and accordingly as Christ finds the heart engaged or disengaged as to things of the wicked world, he becomes thereunto a life or death, a reward or punishment. So he that is to receive this bread of angels in the Holy Sacrament ought to busy himself in discharging his heart from the lumber of worldly affections, and freeing it from all that is earthly; he must do what in him lies to render it worthy of the presence of so divine a guest. This is that purity of a soul which Christ requires, not only the purity of our actions, but of all our affections. We must therefore overcome ourselves, and all our bad inclinations and affections. *Vincenti dabo edere de ligno vitae,* says Christ (Apocalypse 2), "To him, that overcomes himself, I will give to eat of the tree of life." To reap, then, the benefit of this Divine Sacrament, it is necessary that we overcome ourselves, that we subdue our appetites, and our reason to God. Dear Christians, if you will come worthily to eat of this tree of life, down with ambition, humble your pride, away with self-esteem, mortify the desires of vain glory, banish anger, and the spirit of revenge from your heart, overcome your impatience, let not within your heart reign any faintness of spirit, any tepidity in devotion; in a word, vanquish your whole-self, be no more your own but Christ's, abide in Christ. But, that this may be done, it is necessary that whatever you are in yourself should die in you, and Christ only live in you, that you may be able to say with truth: *Vivo ego, iam non ego, vivit vere in me Christus.* (Galatians 2:20)—"I live, now not I, but Christ liveth in me." I am clear now of my self, I have examined my heart, I have cleansed my affections, I have discumbered my soul, thereby to make it a worthy habitation of my God.

The second preparation before Holy Communion is a purity of conscience not only from mortal sin, and all sinful inclinations and affections; but also, as much as possible, from all venial sin, and all affections of venial sin, and all habits of any such sins. Which venial sins, when fully deliberate, hinder the soul very much from being sensible of the heavenly sweetness, and excellent fruits of this Divine Sacrament. Dear Christians, so great a purity is required from us when we go to receive the Divine Majesty within our breasts, that a greater purity is not requisite to see him in his glory, than to receive him in this Sacrament. We ought to be as pure and spotless to receive God in the Sacrament as to see him in heaven. No soul that is impure, or defiled with the least venial sin, can enter into heaven; nothing with imperfection can be admitted into those seats of angels. Nor ought any soul, that is impure or defiled with the least sin, to approach this table of angels, or any thing that is imperfect presume to feed on this Divine Food. The disposition which Christ requires in those who are to see him face to face in his heavenly glory, the disposition is that of a little child. "Unless you become like little ones," say Christ, (Matthew 18), "you shall not enter into the kingdom of heaven." Again Christ says "If any be a little one, let him come unto me," and on this condition let him eat of my bread. So that you see the same disposition is required in those that receive Christ in the Sacrament, as in those that see him in heaven. Nay, if we consider the actions of our Saviour, we shall find that he seems to require a greater and more diligent preparation from us, when we are to receive him in the Sacrament, than we are to see him in glory. In the night of the Last Supper our Saviour washed the feet of all his disciples—"he began to wash the feet of the disciples, and to wipe them with a towel." (John 13)—which was symbolically to wash and cleanse them from all defects, before they fed on this Divine Sacrament. But nothing of this was done by our Saviour to the three of these disciplines, whom he took with him to the Mount Tabor, there to manifest his glory to them in his Transfiguration. Whereby our Saviour gives us to understand, that a greater purity, if possible, is to be procured by us to receive him in the Sacrament, than to see him in glory. Dear Christians, wash then off the spots and sins of your soul in the Sacrament of Confession, before you sitte down at this Divine Banquet. Wash off not only all mortal sins, but even the least venial sin and imperfection, that so feeding on this bread of angels, you yourself may become like angels. For how little soever the sin may be, it is to be washed off before you communicate; all inordinate affections, and all vehemency of passions, are to be purged away. Thus Christ, when he washed the feet of his disciples before the institution and communion of the Holy Sacrament, wiped off the spots of venial sins that adhered to their affections. Attend, Dear Christians, the dignity, where unto you are raised by the Holy Eucharist to be one with God, to be espoused unto God, to be transformed into God; he who worthy communicates abides in God, and God in him. Imitate then, Dear Christians, the purity of the angels, make yourself fit by an innocent and spotless life to receive this bread of life. If you are not pure and innocent, wash off all sins with the cleansing water of penitential tears, and make yourselves fit to receive the true body and blood in the Most Blessed Sacrament.

Finally, Dear Christians, if you desire to prepare in your souls a fit lodging for Jesus Christ, you must not only cleanse your inward house from the dirt and filth of sin, but you must also procure the proper ornaments and furniture of virtue and devotion, that your lodging may be aggreable to the great king that comes to visit you. This is the last preparation before communion. The groundwork of this preparation must be a lively faith, and a serious consideration of the work we are about. We ought to consider who it is that we are to receive; how great a God, how glorious, how pure and holy. And who we are that are going to receive him; how poor and miserable creatures, how wretched and unworthy sinners. We ought to believe with a lively faith that we receive him who is our Maker and our Redeemer, infinite in majesty and infinite in mercy, and who brings with him all the treasures of heaven to enrich us. We ought to believe that we receive the same body of Christ that was conceived by the Holy Ghost and born of the Virgin Mary, the same that was adored in Bethlehem, whose very presence made the devil trouble, whose very touch raised the dead to life, and cured all diseases. The same body of Christ, that was crucified, rose again, and ascended into heaven, and will come to judge both the living and the dead. O think, Dear Christians, with what purity of life and conscience you ought to receive this most blessed body of Christ, which is so much adored both in heaven and upon earth. But what ought to be our sentiments in consequence of our faith of the real presence of Jesus Christ, our Lord and God, in this Blessed Sacrament. O what reverence ought we to bring with us, when we draw near to so tremendous a Majesty, in whose sight the whole creation is a mere nothing? What fear we ought to bring when we enter into his sanctuary, who is infinitely pure and holy, who sees all our guilt, and cannot endure iniquity. What sentiments of humility, when we reflect what he is and what we are! What sorrow and contrition for all our past offences against this infinite Goodness! What sentiments of gratitude for his giving us here his ownself in this wonderful manner! What desires of returning him love for love. O, how would a Christian be affected, if he visibly and evidently saw his God before him in his approaching to this Blessed Sacrament! A lively faith, which apprehends things invisible as if they were visible, would produce the like affections. O, Dear Christians, if we have this lively faith, how ought we to annihilate ourselves in the sight of this great God, and Maker of heaven and earth! How ought we to fear and to tremble, with what profound reverence we ought to approach to the Holy of Holies who lies here concealed under the sacramental veils! But then, lest this fear and reverence should go so far, as to drive us away from this fountain of life, it must be qualified with a humble confidence in the infinite goodness and mercy of him, who invites us to come, and who is ever ready to receive with open arms his prodigal children, when they return to him with a true sense of their unworthiness. Therefore we ought to beg with earnest prayers of this infinite Majesty, that since he knows our great poverty, and inability to prepare him a fit lodging, he himself would prepare one for himself, by sending beforehand those graces and virtues and that fervour of devotion which may fit our souls for him.

Conclusion

I conclude with the words of the church: "O sacred banquet," says the church in the anthem used during this octave! "O sacred banquet, in which Christ is received!" O adorable Sacrament, O Mystery of mysteries! Admire, Dear Christians, the divine power of God therein, who works a thing so far beyond the reach of our understanding! Adore this Goodness and Wisdom in providing for you a spiritual banquet! Praise his mercy and love in making himself the miraculous food of your soul. O Sacred Bread, which comes down from heaven, giving us life everlasting. Submit, Dear Christians, with a humble heart your sense, your reason, your understanding to the almighty power of God in this Divine Mystery. The same omnipotent God, who said at the creation: "Let it be made," now says to you: "This is my body;" and since he has declared himself to be realy present therein, who will dare to say he is not. Exercise yourselves, Dear Christians, before Communion, in acts of faith, reverence, and humility; in acts of hope and confidence in your Saviour; in acts of divine love and in ardent desires after him, accompanied with a grateful remembrance of the love our Saviour has shewed to you, in giving himself to you. And the more you bring with you of this preparation and devotion, the more plentiful will you draw of the waters of Divine grace from this fountain of life. You will draw a life of grace here, and an everlasting life hereafter. Amen.

1762
Pomfret
Walles-neck
Mrs. Elders
Frederick

St. Francis Xavier, Boehmia Manor established by the Jesuits in Cecil County, Maryland in 1704. John Carroll attended the short-lived Bohemia Manor Academy 1746–1748. (Harry Connolly photo)

JOHN BOONE
On the Obligation of the Christian Life
1765

John Boone was born in Prince Georges County, Maryland on April 18, 1735, the son of a prominent Maryland Catholic family. The family chapel, "Boone's Chapel," (still standing) was a regular sub-station of the Jesuit plantation at White Marsh, and in the early nineteenth century became the nucleus for the parish which developed at Rosaryville. Boone was admitted to the Society of Jesus on September 7, 1756. Both his brother, Edward, and his cousin, Joseph, also were members of the Society. Boone initially returned to Maryland on May 31, 1765, and ministered at New-town Manor in St. Mary's County. After five years he returned to England and worked with his brother. He remained in England throughout the American strug-gle for independence, only returning again to Mary-land in 1784. He died at St. Inigoes, Maryland on April 11, 1785.

His sermon, "on the establishment of the Christian Church and obligation of Christian life," was first preached for the feast of St. Francis Xavier, New-town's patronal feast, December 3, 1765, and subse-quently used for the Sixth Sunday after Epiphany.

Newtown, December 3, 1765. *Pro festo S. F. Xaverio.* On
the establishment of the Christian Church and obligation of
Christian life.
6th post Epiphaniam. Ad majorem Dei Gloriam.
Simile est regnum coelorum grano sinapis.

"The kingdom of heaven is like to a grain of mustard
seed."

St. Matthew, chapter 13, verse 31).

By the kingdom of heaven I mean the Church, and state
of Christianity, which from a very small and low beginning,
by degrees, rose and increased to a wonderful height and
greatness. A grain of mustard seed is very small, but sowed
in a warm climate it rises quick, and by its greatness
surpasses all other herbs in its height becoming like a tree,
capable to afford rest and shelter to the birds of the air. No
comparison could give us a more lively or better description
of the beginning and progress of the Church. In the beginning, like the mustard seed, it was very small, but planted
in a warm soil, watered by the hot blood of thousands of
holy marters and cultivated by the labour and zeal of
confessors, it soon increased, spread its goodly branches
round the earth, and invited all nations to repose under its
beautiful shade. I don't doubt but I here bring into your
minds the great St. Francis Xavier whose feast the Church
celebrates today, and whose characteristic it was to have
been created for the glory of God to carry the light of the
Gospellto the remotest corners of the globe. St. Francis'
greatest ambition was to promote the honour and glory of
God by establishing Chrisianity, and carry the sacred rays
of the Gospellto all the corners of the universe. And, as St.
Francis cheerfully aimed at planting the Church, and wa-
terwing it with his sweat and cultivating it with his labours,
I think I can't choose a subject more pleasing to our saint,
and your entertainment, than the establishment of God's

holy Catholic Church upon earth which is my first point; and the indispensable obligation you lie under, as members of the Catholic Church, to live according to the pure and holy maxims of it. These are the two parts which I shall enlarge upon and consider in my ensuing discourse, and to which I beg your favourable attention.

Part 1

Almighty God, speaking to the Jews by the prophet Isaias, says, "my thoughts are not as your thoughts, nor my ways as your ways." In nothing does the truth of this assertion appear more evident and more conspicuous than in the first beginning and planting of the Catholic Church. How did our blessed Saviour bring this about? Was it by human sterngth or power? Was it by arms? Was it by first enslaving their bodies, in order to captivate their minds, that not daring to resist, they might blindly obey his will? No! Nothing of this appears either in his coming into the world or his conduct. The ministers and instruments of this grand design are twelve poor persons, most of them fishermen. The apostles were illiterate men, strangers to that art and address by which great revoltuions have been brought about. They were called from their fishing boats to follow our blessed Saviour, to wait upon him in a life of poverty and hardship. But all their hopes seems quite extinguished by the ignominious death, and passion of their master. They were then left to themselves without help or assistance, exposed and daily apprehensive of falling a sacrifice to the resentment of the Jews, that, as they had shown themselves his disciples as alive, they might soon be made his followers in death. In this melancholy situation were the apostles after the death of Jesus, those who were designed to propagate the Christian faith, and preach it to all the nations of the earth and thereby establish the Catholic Church. Could antyhing in appearance be more unlikely to succeed in such a design with men in these circumstances! But they did not long remain so! The seed was sown in the ground, and, tho small, it quickly rose and began to spread itself. In vain did the enemies of the Christian faith endeavour to stop its progress. It daily gained ground, and by the labours and by the preaching of the apostles and traveling into all parts of the world, by degrees, all nations embraced the faith which triumphed over all the efforts of its enemies. Fire, sword, racks and torments, the severst and most cruel persecutions, under which the Church labourd for 3 hundred years, seemed but to render it more fruitfull. Watered by the warm blood of so many marters, it grew high and spread its branches, till at length it triumphed over idolatry and superstition and became the mistress of the world, by succeeding emperors and kings who doffed their crowns at the foot of the cross and added to their crowns the glory of becoming converts to that faith which had been so cruelly persecuted, and of becoming nursing fathers and protectors of the Church which its enemies had laboured to destroy.

This the small beginning! This the wonderful increase of Christianity. Here, let infidelity own its error! Let modern, bold deriders of revealed religion assign some other cause to this surprising event, of this wonderful propagation and establishment of Christianity. Or, let them confess the divine author of it, that it is the work of God, by his Son, Jesus Christ, who came into the world thus to found the Christian institute, and plant his Catholic Church, with which, according to his promise, he will be to the end of the world. The Church is raised, assisted, and protected by her divine spouse, Jesus Christ, and has maintained herself against the attacks of her more formidable enemies, viz., politicians and new heresies rise up daily against her but she still remains, and ever shall remain, the one, holy Catholic, and apostolic Church of Jesus Christ—one in the constant and immoveable possession of the one same faith taught by Jesus Christ and his apostles; holy, in the admirable sanctity of her doctrines, delivered from the sacred oracles, the word of God; truly catholic, or universal, subsisting in all ages, and sending her holy preachers to all parts of the world; truly apostolical, deriving her orders and mission, and her authority, and spiritual power from Christ, and his apostles, by a continued, uninterrupted succession from them. Still venerable in her sanctity and illustrious in her members, and according to the promise of her divine spouse, shall thus continue to the end of the world. The gates of hell shall never prevail against her. He has said he will be with her to the end, leading and guiding her into all truth. The promises of Christ to his Church may justly be considered the cause of the holy lives of the primitive Christians and first possessors of the Gospell, and of the propgation of Christianity, and its subsisting, as it has done, for so many ages. Promises, I say, made by truth itself, and can never fail, nor be called in question, without contradiciting the veracity of God. It must be astonishing and surprising that any one, who professes to believe the Gospell of Christ, that he is the Son of God, God himself, essentially and invariably here, to deny these promises or suppose them not to be made good. Yet, alas, this is the case of many, who boldly charge the whole Christian world with errors, errors of the worst kind and which destroy the very being of the Church. Christ promised to build his Church upon a rock, and that the gates of hell should not prevail against her. He has done it, and upon the rock she remains and shall continue fixed immoveably to the end of the world, to the consumation of all things.

Here let me, in the bowels of Jesus Christ, the spouse of this his holy Catholic Church, here let me, I say, address myself to you, if any are here present, who have unhappily separated yourselves from her communion! Tell me, O my Christians, but mistaken Christians, why, O why have you thus deserted and forsaken her, who first brought you forth to Christ and his Gospell. Why, O why have you rent and tore the seamless coat of Christ, your common Saviour and redeemer. O tell me, I beseech you, a sign, a sufficient cause for this your unhappy separation! A separation, the consequences of which makes me grive, makes me fear, and tremble. I tremble for so many souls redeemed by the pretious blood of Jesus. Tell me, I say freely, and with the same spirit of charity with which I put the question, with all deference to your learning, your posts, and your persons! Will you say, the Church has fallen into, and been at once drowned in abominable living, idolatry, to the destruction and subversion of all good religion. If this is your answer, I thus reply, and tell you that the Church of God has ceased to be a Church; that the gates of hell have prevailed against her! And that divine truth himself has not kept his word, and promise to her. But is there a Christian who believes in Christ, and who does not shudder and tremble at such a supposition as this! Christ promised to send his Holy Spirit, the spirit of truth to lead and guide her into all truth. He has done this and continually assisted by this spirit, she cannot teach her children false doctrine, nor err in matters of faith. I speak boldly here, ye novilists, ye modern reformers of the Church's faith! I speak boldly and dare to say, Christ's promises are not to be relied on. O my God! To what extravagant and monstrous lengths will the pride, vanity, and infidelity, and the itch of novilty carry themselves! Christ assured his Church he himself would be with her even to the end of the world. He will be so; and governed and assisted by his presence, she is, and ever will remain the pillar and ground of truth. Christ cannot, will not be false to his word. His word endrues for ever. Heaven and earth shall pass away but his word shall never pass away. Had these promises of Christ to his Church been duly attended to, and seriously considered, pride, and self conceit, and any other unwarrantable motive, had never caused so many of her children in different ages, and at different times, to rise up against their spiritual mother the Church, and tear her seamless coat by heresies, schisms, and an ill grounded separation from her holy communion! So many unhappy souls had not been lost by forsaking the plain Church way to truth, to follow the blind guides of their own private judgements and fancies, in opposition to her unerring authority. As the Church, by these illustrious promises, has maintained herself, against all the efforts of hereticks, separatists, and novelists, so nothing could or would conduce more effectually to unite all Christians again in the same faith than seriously to consider these promises thus made to the Church by Christ. It is these glorious promises which may, and ought to be considered as one reason to be assigned for the firm establishment and perpetuity of the Christian religion which the devine author of it has so strongly, as I may say, engaged himself to support and maintain. From these mentioned causes sprung this wonderfull event. Thus the kingdom of Christ, like the grain of mustard seed, daily increased. May it still grow and further increase, till all nations once more hasten to repose under the cover of its shade. May those burning and shining lights once more appear, to dispell the darkness of that infidelity wherein so many be immersed. May Jews, Turks, pagans, and infidels hear and oboey the voice of Christ, the true shepherd of souls, and hast to enter into his saveing fold, the Church! May all who live in error or mistake be corrected by that sure rule and only safe guide. I believe one holy, Catholic and apostolical Church. And may all Christians, who glory in the name, endeavour to imitate their primitive ancestors, in the purity and holiness of their lives, as they do in the profession of the same Catholic faith. Having thus considered the rise and progress of the Church and state of Christianity, I shall now lay before you the obligation you lie under, as members of the Catholic Church, to live according to the faith you profess.

To boast of a Christian name, and to dishonour it by an

unchristian life! To glory in being members of the Catholic Church, and to dishonour that holy profession, by living like heathens and infidels, is highly criminal and equally surprising. As the Church's faith is invariable, as the Gospell precepts are the same now as they were in the beginning, and equally obligatory, Christianity is the same, no other, as it was in the primitive times, and you are as much obliged to live like Christians now as they were then. The empty name of a Christian will be of no service, or advantage to you. It will live, only for the greater condemnation of those, who have no more of the Christian than the heathen. If you think, to separate faith from good works, a belief in Jesus Christ from obeying his commands, you deceive yourselves. The illusion is gross, and the consequences of it very dreadfull, however you may flatter yourselves with mistaken notions. If you do not live like Christians, if you do not show that your lives correspond to your profession, you may be stiled practical unbelievers, and your portion will be with heathens and infidels. The only difference will be you will undergo a more severe judgement, and be more rigorously punished, and justly. For what will the glorious light of the Gospell serve, if you love darkness rather than light. For what purpose have you been brought up in the glorious liberty of the children of God if you make yourselves slaves of sin and run again into that bondage from whence you have been freed. These reflections, as they naturally occur, they'll discover to you such truths of importance as to deserve your utmost and serious attention. You are a Christian, a member of God's holy Catholic Church! Here you must see unless you are willfully blind, obstinately perverse, you must, I say, see your duty and obligation. That you are bound to live like a Christian, vy the spirit of the Gospell; that as you deviate from this in your conduct, so far are you from being what you profess yourdelf to be. You must confess that if you do not live like a Christian, you do, in effect, deny Jesus

Christ, and that all your hopes to salvation thro him are vain and groundless, since he himself has told you so. Not every one who says to me, Lord, Lord, shall enter into the kingdom of heaven, but he who does -he will of my father who is in heaven. Hence it evidently appears that the Christian religion is a practical one, that its design is chiefly to regulate your morals, and not only to inform your understanding by its speculative truths, but to reform the corrupt morals of man and to bring him to the practice of virtue and holiness. Hence the character of a Christian is beautifully given by the great Saint Cyprian, *non magna loquirmus, sed vivimus.* We don't affect to speak fine things, but to live well. This is the sum of our duty, to live well by the practicing the virtues preached and and related to us in the gospel. Faith is absolutely necessary; without it, as the apostles observes, it is impossible to please God. Right and true faith in the holy mysteries of the Christian religion is the foundation, or basis, on which our spiritual building is to be raised, but good works and a holy life are the parts which constitute this building. Unless the super-structure of practical piety is raised upon the foundation of faith, that faith will be unprofitable to us; faith without works is dead. Christianity is a practical religion, and we fall short of our duty if we do not practice virtue and holiness, without which one shall not see God. How far do you not deviate from your profession while you live in sin and the transgression of God's commands is obvious to every one. It is clear that in this case you deceive your-selves. You are not what you call yourselves, and therefore, you must expect to be treated as enemies to the faith which, though you profess it with your lips, you deny it by your actions. While you give thanks to Almighty God as you ought to do, for bringing you to the knowledge and profes-sion of the Christian religion, while you glory in being members of the Catholic Church, let your lives show you are Christians. Let the maxims of the gospel you profess have a due influence over your conduct, that no one may approach you for contradicting your profession. "So let your light shine before men," says Jesus Christ, "that they may see your good works and gloridy your heavenly father who is in heaven." This every Christian is obliged to do in that station wherein God has placed him. Great is the power of good example. Nothing recommends virtue more efficatiously than the practice of it. Religion appears in all its charms, able to subdue the most obdruate heart, when it is enforced by the powerful persuasion and conviction of good example. By this method it may once more triumph over all its oppressors. The attempt is glorious, and it will not be found so difficult. Every one may contribute to it, and bring it about. Let every one be persuaded that practical religion is that alone which will save him, and you will all find it as much your interest as it is your duty seriously to labour for it. Let this, my brethren, be the subject of serious thoughts and reflections, and may the grace of God inspire you with a sincere desire and assist you in your serious endeavours to live as becomes the children of the religion you profess, that you may one day happily partake of the glorious reward it is promised you in the next life to be. Amen.

Soli Deo gloria.

JOHN BOLTON

John Bolton was born in England on October 22, 1742 and entered the society of Jesus at Watten, Flanders, on September 7, 1761. After ordination in 1771, he was sent to the Maryland Mission, being first posted in Charles County. In September, 1787 he succeeded Joseph Mosley at St. Joseph's on the Eastern Shore of Maryland, and continued Mosley's fruitful ministry in lower Maryland and Delaware, making many converts among both blacks and whites. He is listed as coming to Newtown, Maryland in April, 1802, and died there in the autumn of 1809.

The longer sermon for the Feast of Mary's Assumption touches on the heavenly glorification of Mary and her usefulness as an advocate. It is cited as having been delivered at the Charles County sub-stations of Newport, Sakia (present Waldorf) and Port Tobacco, and later at St. Joseph's in Talbot County. Interspersed with this sermon is another sermon for the same feast, preached at the sub-stations of Newport and Cornwallis in 1780 and 1786, which stresses the efficacy of praying the Rosary. The sermon on paying honor to the saints appears to have been the third in a series of sermons on the Ten Commandments. Askmore would appear to refer to a 550 acre plantation adjacent to Bohemia Manor which was purchased by the Jesuits in 1732. It is unclear whether the 1789 citation "F. Charles Car." refers to the home of the Maryland Catholic signer of the Declaration of Independence. The sermon on the Eucharist was first preached at St. Joseph's on the Eastern Shore in 1799, and later used at Medley's Neck, a sub-station of Newtown Manor in St. Mary's County in 1802.

JOHN BOLTON
The Assumption of Mary
1772

Newport 1772
Sakia 1773
Port Tobacco 1784
St. Joseph's 1789
Do. 1797

"The Queen stood on thy right hand in gilded clothing surrounded with variety." (Psalm 44: 11).

Assumpta est Maria in colum. Mary is assumed into heaven. (Words taken out of the Introit of Mass.)

It being to day the feast of the Virgin's Assumption, no doubt, Christians, you expect I should say something in praise of this glorious queen, the world's empress and mother to no less a person than a God incarnate. Indeed had I my own choice, I had rather invite you to a tacit admiration of this glorious assumption, than to a publick declaration of what can never be sufficiently manifested or expressed according to its worth, dignity, and merit. The subject is both ample and great. And to use St. Bernard's expression, "tho there is nothing which delights me more than to speak of this glorious queen, yet at the same time I am dismayed of discourse of this so admirable a subject." It delights me because, as the saint says, she is the very fountain, offspring and source from whence flows the author and aim of all our happiness here and hereafter. I am dismayed seeing she is an immense sea of praises as the very signification of the Virgin's name sufficiently declares and knowing it to be out of the power of man not only to adorn, but even in the least king to adumbrate so glorious and noble a triumph as St. Basil expresses it. *Qui omnia illustria et gloria dixerit, dignitatis magnitudinem nulla umquam oratione adequabit*. I shall at least content myself with this, that she is a most bening mother and looks not upon what we say so much, as she regards the will and intention wherewith we do it and therefore will endeavor to say something of the Solemnity as well to animate your zeal for the honor of the Mother of God as to increase your love and esteem for her, by laying before you the glory which accrues to Our Lady, as also the profit that redounds to us by her glorious assumption. Such is our present subject drawn chiefly from such holy Fathers as were her most faithful clients here on earth. To which I beg the favour of your attention by saluting her together with the celestial hierarchy, *Hail Mary*.

In it a query of the mellifluous dear St. Bernard upon the words of St. Paul, that as God has prepared so great a reward (as neither eye has seen, nor ear has heard nor has descended into the heart of man) for those that love him, what may we think has He not prepared for her, who not only loved but conceived, carried and nourished in her sacred womb the God of eternal power, majesty and glory. And as it is incomparable which she bore, ineffable which she conceived, so certainly must be inconceivable the reward of her eternal greatness. What tongue then shall we find able to declare? What mind sufficient to comprehend? What human understanding able to express with what joy, jubily and content the degrees of celestial souls go forth to meet their queen and empress; with what splendour they present her to the throne of glory, and with what divine embraces she was received by her Son and exalted above all creatures according to her worth and merit. Here it is that St. Peter Damian sticks not to affirm that this Assumption of Our Lady was far more stately, glorious and set out with greater pomp, than was the Ascension of Christ our Saviour; and alledges this pious and forceable reason, that in the Ascension of Christ his concomitancy was only made up of pious souls and angels. But in the Assumption of our

Virgin not only saints and angels, but the King of both
Saints and Angels, the Sun of Justice, the God of Majesty,
the Prince of Glory, whose dignity is infinite, whose immensity unmeasurable and whose greatness is boundless,
came forth in company of all just souls, angels, and the
court of heaven to conduct her to the Eternal Father as his
daughter, to welcome her as his mother, and present her to
the Holy Ghost as his spouse and darling. This triumph
then, O glorious Virgin, has not only elevated you to so
eminent a degree of glory, but also it has adorned heaven
itself with a new splendour and all things therein contained
with a new light and beauty, because your arrival irradiated
with the dignity of your transcendent virtues and illumi-
nated it as it were with the light of your superabundant
graces. I seem to myself to behold with what glory and
splendour you pass by the choir of angels, surmount the
hierarchies of blessed souls and leave behind you all those
inferior orbes of heavenly spirits. For as the mother of the
Eternal Word it is no ways fitting you should take up your
abode amongst angels or inferior creatures. No, a particular
choir, a singular hierarchy is more suitable and becoming
your majesty and glory, a hierarchy never to be sufficiently
admired, which is, as it were, the very sum and compen-
dium of all the rest how many soever united and combined
together; for whatsoever of grace, glory and goodness we
see dispersed amongst others by parcels, here we behold it
collected as it were into its proper treasury and center.
Here, dear congregation, by the by, give me leave to remind
you of one thing, no one must imagine that these expressions or elogium given Our Lady to be too sublime or any
ways derogating from the honour and glory due to the
Almighty, since the holy fathers and the Church speak of
her in this manner, but in an inferior degree, only as a pure
creature invested with all manner of gifts and graces superior to those of all the saints and angels and which by her
exceeding great dignity in quality of Mother of God she had

an undoubted right to; for pray what mortal, what creature, what angel has ever been able to say with the Eternal Father, *Filius meus es tu, ego genui te.* "You are my son, I have begotten you," but this our Virgin, this our glorious queen, and only she is able to affirm, she only with verity may boldly assert it. This immense dignity then of Mother of God must of necessity place her in the highest throne, this elevate her to the supermost hierarchy and place her at the right hand of her Son where she may behold only that ever Blessed Trinity above her and look upon all the choirs of angels and saints in heaven far beneath her. Thrice happy day then may I call this which has seated our glorious Lady where she enjoys a paradise of pleasure, where she takes a view of the most ample and illustrious company of angels, the most adorned assembly of patriarchs, and of her Son crowned with infinite honour and glory, cloathed with light as with a vestment governing the world by his infinite power, wisdom and majesty. In a word she beheld herself exalted above all the choirs of celestial spirits and seated in great majesty and glory above all things created. Thus we have considered Mary raised to a most eminent degree of glory; we admire her, thus glorified, yet it must not be absolutely and precisely because she was the Mother of God, but because she had been obedient and faithful to God, because she had been humble in the sight of God, and by reason of these two qualities had rendered herself in a singular manner and by excellence the handmaid of God and arrived at so elevated degree of happiness. However possessed as she is of such glory she is ever mindful of us, will be ever sensible of our wants and miseries, and is now become a more than ever powerful protectrine and advocate in our behalf, the subject of my second point.

It would be wrong to imagine the sublime state which the Blessed Virgin is raised to any ways hinders her from looking down upon us. On the contrary her glory makes her more solicitous and attentive to our wants and necessities. For if she ever felt inclined to give unto man some token of her sovereign power it certainly must be today in which she takes full possession. So that I may safely add with a certain pious author that if it was violence and an effort of the love of God which separated her soul from her body to take flight to that happy mansion, the love she bore to us mortal men was an additional force to her hastening thither, to the end she might serve us in quality of mother and protectrine and next to God become our greatest hope. But what do we conclude from hence? We have a mother so powerful who has so much love for us and yet remain in misery and want; oppressed with temptations, attacked and perchance overcome with all manner of vice and hardly ever call upon her assistance. We don't know certainly how to reap benefit from her favour and protection. *Accedamus cum fiducia ad thronum gratia ejus,* cries out one of her favourites in the words the Apostle said to Our Saviour; let us approach with confidence to this throne of grace where mercy pleads for us and takes our part. It is not a throne from whence God darts lightning upon sinners but from whence He displays his mercy, a throne of grace where our crimes are washed away; for as she, whilst on earth, was the throne in which God took more delight in dwelling than in any other place, so now in heaven she is appointed the throne for the azilum or refuge of sinners who therefore must not be afraid to approach to her provided they have an efficacious desire to quit their disorderly ways. Yes, Christians, says St. Bernard, we have the most holy Virgin for advocate with her Son as we have Jesus Christ for advocate with his Father. Who can doubt then but Mary, being the mother of our supreme judge, a mother most beloved, most holy, a mother crowned with glory, who can doubt, but she will meet with a favourable audience and plead our cause successfully out of respect as I may say to her maternity. Yes, adds the same saint speaking of the Virgin's Assumption, tho that lady is departed, that queen

is gone, that advocate has left us, who on earth gave so
many signs of her love, so many testimonies of her assistance and so many proofs of her good will and affection
toward us, yet considering the immense profit that accrues
to us we have far greater reason to rejoice than to condole
her departure; for our exile and peregrination has so before
it an advocate who knows how to deal both suppliantly and
efficaciously the affairs of our security being as well the
judge's mother as Mother of Mercy. Great we must confess
to have been the Virgin's power even whilst she lived
amongst us, but far greater must we acknowledge it to be
now whilst she reigns in the celestial kingdom, for now it
appears most evidently she shows far greater clemency and
innumerable more benefits to mankind, as being in a capacity of beholding far more apparently the manifold miseries
to which we are exposed and the innumerable trouble to
which we are liable and the number of afflictions to which
we are subject. It is reported in the Third Book of Kings,
second chapter, that Bersabe being about to ask a favour
of her son, King Solomon for Adonia, he made this dutiful
and obedent answer: "Ask mother what you please, neither
will it stand with justice that you receive denial." And can
we ever persuade ourselves that Christ who is goodness
itself, author of all gifts and favours, will be less kind to his
loving mother than Solomon was to his mother, Bersabe,
and that Christ will not grant her all her petitions since
whatever she asks is just, holy and reasonable. We know
likewise in Holy Writ that King Assueras told Queen Esther
that altho she should petition one half of his kingdom, she
should not be frustrated of her desire but obtain whatever
she asked for. And yet this is but a shadow of that free will,
liberality and greatness the King of Kings is pleased to
show the Virgin, his Mother, when she pleases to interceed
in our behalf. We have them without all question a powerful
advocate by having both the Queen of Heaven and the
judge's mother, to whom is given great power both in

heaven and earth and all authority suitable to her dignity and office. Whence St. Peter Damian: "How can that power give repulse to your intercession which drew its origin from your holy body and took its beginning from your sacred bowels." Let us then seek mercy and seek it by means of the Virgin. Whoever does invocate by so powerful a means, undoubtedly will obtain his request, because the Son will hear his mother, her greatness will meet with a favourable grant and facile audience. If you dare not appear before that dreadful majesty of God himself or fear to have recourse to the terrible judge, at least you may with confidence approach to the sacred Virgin, the very object of lenity, mildness and mercy, a title she so much glories in and which of all others most properly belongs to her.

What now remains since in some sort we have seen the glory of this holy Virgin and beheld in some manner her powerful assistance, but that we congratulate with her for her dignity and with ourselves for so glorious an advocate. Since all the choirs of angels and blessed spirits exult and rejoice at this glorious triumph. Enjoy, then, O glorious Virgin, that happiness your Son has prepared for you, possess the reward of your merits, rest now secure from all care, affliction and misery. You are in a secure possession of never loosing that bliss, and in the true security of ever retaining that happiness, joy and comfort of which you are now partaker. But, forget not, O happy Virgin, forget not poor mortals in the midst of your jubily and triumph. Cast a merciful eye, one favourable glance upon these your clients in this vail or misery. You are in a secure possession of eternal happiness, we in the midst of a thousand dangers. We beg your succour, we entreat your aid and implore your assistance. We have framed to ourselves some notion of your power and greatness and acknowledge our own weakness and misery. Show yourself to be a mother and a mother of mercy and obtain for us grace of your Blessed Son, that by virtuous and edifying lives, we may henceforward be stiled your children, to the end we may one day deserve to enjoy your happy company, together with all the saints and angels in eternal bliss. Amen.

JOHN BOLTON
The Rosary
1780

Assumption
Newport 1780
Cornwallis 1786

Astitit Regina a dextris tuis.
"The Queen, thy mother, was placed at thy right hand."
(Psalm 44).

As the Church celebrates to day the feast of the Assumption of the Blessed Virgin, it would not be improper to speak of some devotions to her, and see what are the exceptions against them, and what the abuses in them. And of all these whatever they be, we lay down this as a general ground for coming to a good understanding, that none of them, however approved, are enjoined by the Church and so far from being made a term of communion, that all the members of it are at full liberty of using them if they think fit, and likewise of letting them alone.

Now in particular as to the Rosary on beads, it is certain they are approved and are serviceable to piety, if and according to the direction of those books which prescribe the method; by leading the mind thro all the misteries of man's Redemption and giving it a frequent opportunity of a grateful acknowledgement of all that God has done for us. They may in particular be helpful to such as cannot read, or are any ways disabled from the use of a book. Since by these, a person may at any time employ half an hour in prayer without any burthen of memory, who otherwise would be at a loss of spending five minutes. This is many times a help even to the learned, who having their minds tired with books, or being desirous to walk, have in these a method of making addresses to God; but a much greater help to the ignorant, in being thus provided of a means of being as constant, and spending as much time in prayer, as those who have the best choice of books. And what this advantage is, those may easily imagine, who know how dull and barren are the minds of the unlearned, and how soon they are at a stand where they even intend to turn their hearts to God. This convenience must be acknowledged considerable, but then when the thing is enquired into, and it appears, that in using the beads, persons pray ten times more to the Virgin Mary, than to God, this overthrows all again, and makes the advantage of such prayers to be worse than not praying at all. This description of the beads, I confess, has no encouragement in it, as far as it seems to insinuate a greater application to, and more confidence in the Blessed Virgin than in God; but this account is not true.

In the first place, because when I desire the Blessed Virgin to pray to God for me, I in this acknowledge, that He is the fountain of all good; and in asking the Virgin Mary to pray to Him for me is only owning her a creature, desiring her to be petitioner with me, and consequently acknowledging, that God's gifts are not in hers, but in his own hands. As often then as I repeat, "Holy Mary, Mother of God, pray for me," it can't be truly said, that I pray to the Blessed Virgin and not to God; for certainly I pray more to God than to her. For see, when I desire a friend, or any just man on earth, to pray for me, is it not with hopes that God will hear him and Grant what I want? Is not my hope in God, my expectation from God, my desire on God? And is not my petition made to God, while I desire my friend to pray for me? Or can it with truth be said, that my desires and requests are more directed to him, than to God; or that I pray to him and not to God? The case is here plain, that as often as I desire another to pray for me, so often do I express my dependence on God, and so often in effect do I pray to him. It's the same thing when I desire the like of the Blessed Virgin, for all that I ask of her, is to be petitioner to God for me, and here my prayer is as much directed to God and my petition is to the King when I desire another to deliver it to him and to make an interest for me. Altho therefore I should say a thousand times together "Holy Mary, pray for me," it is not true that I pray more to the Virgin Mary than to God, because every time I ask it, I pray to God, and expect the grant of my petition from him.

Secondly because when we desire the Blessed Virgin to pray for us, it is not because we have a greater confidence in her than in God; no, God forbid, this is what we utterly abhor as blasphemy itself; but because we have a greater confidence in her prayers than in our own. We know ourselves to be unhappy sinners, and this of our unworthyness makes us fear lest our petition be rejected; here you see is a distrust of ourselves and where is the fault of this, if it be the effect of humility and not of despair? If then, as by God's order, Job's friends were commanded to desire Job to pray for them because he was just and more acceptable to God than they, so we solicit those to pray for us, who are just and more acceptable in God's sight than ourselves, wherein I no ways give them a preference to God, but only to ourselves, hoping that their prayers will more prevail than our own. And now, if ten times together we repeat, "Holy Mary, pray for us," there can be no more inferred from hence, but that we so often express a distrust of ourselves and that we think her prayers more likely to be heard than ours. And what more is this than in the Israelites desiring Moses or Samuel to pray for them, because they hope God would be favorable to their requests, as being more just than themselves.

But what means the so frequent repetition of the same prayer? I answer; if the prayer be good what can be the harm of repeating it? Can persons in distress be reproved for often calling for help? Perseverance and importunity in prayer, and praying always are commended in the Scriptures; and can it be imagined, that God will not have regard to such perseverance, except it has variety to recommend it? This seems a thought beneath the infinite goodness of God, who, prescribing us to pray, has no where declared that unless we have a great change of prayers, he will not hear us. Variety may be some help to us in making us more attentive to what we say; but as to God I cannot comprehend upon what head, variety will more engage him to our assistance, or why the *Lord's Prayer* or even those three words, "thy will be done," repeated for the whole life, may not be as acceptable as any collection of the greatest variety whatever. If repetition be nothing but a formality or custom, I make no defense for it; but if it be the expression of an humble and contrite heart, or of a soul importuning heaven for relief, I think there can be no exception against it, but by absurdily fixing on God the weakness of man and making him subject to "nauseat," where there is not change or intermission of time to prevent it. If a soul were for six hours together under that one thought of desiring mercy, would this take off the value of his prayer? And would it alter the case if that one thought were so often expressed and repeated in words? This has too much to shaping God to our own imagination, and therefore I leave it.

But the sodalities and confraternities, you'll say, under the protection of the Blessed Virgin are not to be so past by, in which Christians list and oblige themselves to her service, and are taught to have so great a confidence in her as not to fear damnation whatever their life be, so they be but constant in their devotion to her. The confraternities here hinted at are most of them approved and being a voluntary engagement of pious persons in frequenting the sacraments, in prayer and fasting and the material assistance of one another can deserve no censure. But if there be any such abuses, as now mentioned in them, I know of no article of any faith, that obliges me to defend them; but

my faith teaches me to condemn them. For does not the
Church teach us from the Gospel to forsake our evil ways,
to deny ourselves, to crucify the flesh with its lusts, if we
desire mercy and expect pardon of sin? If then any are
found that set up for an easier way, pretending to be
assured of salvation upon the ceremony of what they wear
or the formality of some prayers without quitting their
criminal life, they deceive themselves and set up without
quitting their criminal life, they deceive themselves and set
up another gospel against Christ's, and, therefore, can
there be no difficulty in pronouncing, that however, in their
circumstances they desire the Blessed Virgin to pray for
them, she has an abhorrence of all their devotions. Since it
is impossible they who live in the displeasure of God by
their wickedness should be acceptable to the saints, who
cannot be honoured where God is dishonoured? The divers
bishops have declared those histories as false, which give
occasion to such abuses, by representing the Blessed Virgin
more compassionate than her Son, and that she had re-
prieved some of her devotees whom He would have condemned for their wickedness.

Hence we are to conclude that it is necessary for every
one to keep firm to the faith of the Catholick Church, which
teaching that it is pious and profitable to desire the Blessed
Virgin and other saints to pray for us, likewise teaches it to
be absolutely necessary to place our confidence in Jesus
Christ, because as the Scripture declares, there is no salvation but through him, and no other name under heaven
by which we can be saved, but his alone. And therefore
that our principal devotion ought to be to Jesus Christ, who
having delivered himself to death for our sins, continues in
heaven to be our perpetual advocate to the Father. Finally
since Jesus Christ has declared that however devout we are
to him in calling him "Lord, Lord," we cannot enter into
heaven if we do not the will of his Father, we ought to
entertain no hopes of salvation, whatever our devotion be

to the Blessed Virgin and the saints, if we do not repent of our sins, as God has ordained and quitt all our evil ways, to live such true Christians as the Gospel requires.

JOHN BOLTON
Mary and the Saints
1779

The commandments 3
Askmore 1779
F. Charles Car. 1789

Si quis ministraverit honorificabit cum Pater meus.
"If anyone serves me, my Father will honour him."
(John 12).

The worship of the saints is no ways contrary to the first
commandment; it is rather a natural consequence and, as I
may say, inseparable from the honour this commandment
obliges us to pay to God. We can therefore and ought to
honour the saints; it would be doing them an injustice to
refuse them an honour the Church has all along agreed to.
We may also show due honour and respect to their pictures
and reliques which remind us of their holy lives and virtues.
Neither is there any thing herein that can any way justify
our adversaries who reproach the Catholic Church of the
sin of idolatry in honouring the saints, their pictures, and
relicks. The clearing up of this point shall make the subject
of this discourse. Be pleased to favour me with your usual
attention.

The worship of saints, which the Church in all ages has
admitted of, is founded on Scripture. "If anyone serves
me," says Jesus Christ, "my father will honour him;" *si
quis mihi ministraverit etc*. The Royal Prophet speaking of
this worship sticks not to tell Almighty God that his friends
are too much honoured. *Nimis honorate sunt amici tu
Deus*. (Psalm 138). Now God's friends are no other than
the saints, who have been faithful here on earth in doing
his will and keeping his commandments and whom He
himself has stiled such. *Vos amici mei estis, si feceritis*

quod ego precipio vobis. (John 15). Whence it follows that if the great King of Heaven and Earth, if God himself is pleased to honour the saints it is a thing unquestionable that we ought likewise to honour them.

But in what manner are we to honour them? We honour the Blessed Virgin as being the Mother of God and as having by means of so sublime a dignity attained to an intimate union with God, a union, next to the hypostatic union, the most intimate and greatest that could be confered on a pure creation. What I mean by the hypostatic union is that of the second person of the Blessed Trinity, with human nature. The Blessed Virgin, then, being so closely united to God, it follows that if we must honour God, we must also honour his most Blessed Mother, since all honour given her redounds to God himself. In like manner we honour the other saints as servants and friends of God, now elevated in glory and forever united unto him. Thus it is we honour God himself in the person of his saints, and acknowledge him as the sole author of all the gifts and graces we admire in them. We honour, says St. Jerome *(53 Epistle to Riperius),* the relics of martyrs in order to adore him for whose sake they suffered and became martyrs; we honour the servants, that thereby the honour shewed them may redound to their master. What greater allusion then to believe, as some do, that Almighty God is offended at the honour we pay his saints. For just as a king or earthly prince is not offended by seeing those honoured whom he has made partakers of his authority and grandeur, so in like manner God is well pleased when we honour the saints, it being only with reference to him and because He has placed them in the rank of the blessed in a happy eternity.

However there is yet a wide difference betwixt the worship given to God and what is payed to the Blessed Virgin and the saints. The worship given to God consists in acknowledging and adoring him as the creator, lord, and sovereign master of the universe and is called latry; the worship given to the Blessed Virgin is called hiperduly and as far surpasses that honour and worship given the saints, as she by her eminent dignity of Mother of God and by the most singular favours and graces she has received is raised above all the choirs of saints and angels. The worship whereby we honour the saints as servants and and frame to oneself some notion of what our Blessed Saviour suffered on the Cross and with little reflection call to mind with the apostle to what a degree he loved us as to die and suffer in the manner he did for us. *Delexit me et tradidit semetipsum pro me*. (Galatians 2). And naturally speaking whilst the object is represented to us, it makes impression, works in the soul a lively remembrance so that we find some willingness to shew some acknowledgement by exterior signs and by bending the knee or bowing of the head testify the pious sentiments of the heart so moving a sight is apt to excite in us.

The images of the saints make us call to mind the miracles and wonders God has been pleased to work by their means, by the holiness of their lives and actions. They move us also to bless and glorify God, who is admirable in his saints, according to the Royal Prophet in the 67th Psalm, *Mirabilis Deus in sanctis suis;* amd imitate the example of virtue given us throughout the course of their holy lives. Thus for example the picture of St. Peter or St. Mary Magdalen, who bewail their sins, excite us to deplore our own and do penance. That of St. Martin, St. Elizabeth, famous for alms, moves us to support and assist the needy and miserable and so of the rest.

We come at length to the worship the Catholic Church bestows on the relicks of saints. Every one knows that by the relicks of saints is understood their bodies or certain parts thereof, such as the head, leg, arm, bones, their cloathes and whatever may be of them. The worship and honour given the relicks of the saints is very ancient and due to them for divers reasons. First, because the saints' bodies have been so many victims offered to God thro martyrdom or patience and were subservient to the practice of many good works. Secondly because their bodies will one day be united to their happy souls to which as they had been in friends of God is called duly. Besides both the one and the other of these two latter kinds of worship are of inferior sort and only respectable in as much as they are refered to God; hence, we see that by honouring the saints we honour and worship God himself.

To say something of the worship given to the images and pictures of the saints, it naturally follows that as we are obliged to honour the saints, due respect and honour also should be given to their images as thereby represented unto us. This the Council of Trent has explicitly decided, when in the 25th Session, speaking of the invocation of the saints and their images, says that due honour and veneration should be given them. *Imaginibus debitum honorem et venerationem impertiendam.* But not to be under a mistake we must here take particular notice, that whatever be the honour or veneration shewn to images, we are not for that to believe any extraordinary virtue or divinity contained in them as to themselves which challenges our worship; we ask no grace or favour of them; we place no confidence in them as did the idolaters in their idols. Thus, for example, when we honour the image of an apostle or martyr, our intention is not to honour the image itself, but the apostle or martyr there represented. In a word, the honour given to images is refered Jesus Christ, to the Blessed Virgin, and the saints they remind us of and which only as they serve to raise the mind to heaven, there to honour Jesus Christ, his most holy mother, and the saints, and in the saints God himself and the author of all graces and sanctification.

Here it would not be amiss to explain in short the usefulness of images. The images of Jesus Christ put us in mind of his sufferings, of the misteries wrought for our salvation. They inspire devotion, good sentiments and the practice of a devout life. At the sight of the crucifix one may easily conceive this life instrumental in the practice of good works, will also be made partakers of their recompense. Thirdly because these relicks are the precious remnants of bodies which have been living members of Jesus Christ and temples of the Holy Ghost and have born and glorified God to use the words of St. Paul, *glorificate et portate Deum in corpore vestro*. (I to Timothy, 6). [This citation probably should read I Corinthians 6].

In fine what ought strongly to move us to honour the relicks of the saints is the example of God himself, who first honoured them by working many miracles and wonders in their favour. Many instances hereof may be met with in Scripture. In the Fourth Book of Kings, Chapter 13, mention is made of a dead person raised to life by a touch of the corpse of the Prophet Elizee. The very shadow of St. Peter as the Acts of the Apostles (Chapter 5) testify, cured many sick persons laid out in the highway where he passed by and in the same place, tis said, the linnen and handkerchiefs that had touched the body of St. Paul, applied to divers sick people crued and delivered them from the wicked spirits. We may add to these miracles of Holy Writ many others recounted by the holy fathers wrought by the application of saints' relicks in their time. St. Austin in his work called *The City of God,* recalls that a blind woman recovered her sight by only rubbing her eyes with some flowers that had touched the relicks of the holy martyr St. Stephen. Numberless other miracles might be here mentioned were it needful; but I leave it to the sentiments of every unprejudiced, well-thinking person whether we have no sufficient reason, from the reading or hearing these and like wonders, to say with the holy prophet, *Mirabilis Deus in sanctis suis*. (Psalm 67). "God is wonderful in his saints." Have we not the greatest reason to be assured that a respect and veneration shewn to the saints' relicks is authorized by Almighty God, since by these precious remnants He is pleased from time to time to work so great wonders. What a rash and daring attempt then it is in some of our different adversaries to condemn and find fault with a worship God himself has authorized by so many standing miracles, void of all suspicion and founded on the most authentic testimony.

Let us then, Dear Christians, Ever hold in veneration the saints' relicks, a devotion very acceptable to heaven and which has been oftentimes blessed with singular favours. It is for this reason our Holy Mother, the Church has from all times greatly encouraged and approved of pilgrimages, that is, repairing to those holy places and churches in Catholic countries where the saints bodies and relicks were deposited. But after all, in all these and such like devout practices we must chiefly have at heart our own spiritual good and eternal welfare. The intent of them is chiefly to help us in going through courageously with the duties of a Christian life and to sweeten by the many blessings that attend them, the difficulties met with in the service of Christ and therefore to deserve, in some manner, these helps, we must be constantly on our guard to know our duty, God's will, to comply with it, to keep the commandments and abstain from all wilful excesses in any kind. By this means we shall please Almighty God, please the saints and deserve to have them interpose on our behalf. Let us again take notice that to honour the saints and reverence their images as thereby resembled and represented to us as we ought, we must be trying to imitate their virtues, laying before us their holy lives for a sample and pattern, to copy after, this must be our only intent, the only fruit we are to propose to ourselves in honouring them. Almighty God has given them to us as a model of our whole life and conduct as St. Ambrose affirms, *Sanctorum vita ceteri est vivendi forma.* May it please heaven that touched with the example of the saints and forming to ourselves a generous resolution to imitate them, we may one day have the happiness to be of their company and possess Almighty God with them for a whole eternity. Amen.

St. Joseph's, Cordova (Tuckahoe), Talbot County, Maryland. The church incorporates part of the house built by Jesuit Joseph Mosley in 1765. (Harry Connolly photo)

JOHN BOLTON
The Eucharist and the Church
1799

St. Joseph's 1799
Medley's Neck 1802
Festum Corporis Christi 1807

"He that eateth my flesh and drinketh my blood hath everlasting life . . . . for my flesh is meat indeed."

John 6: 55

Thus was the Saviour of the world pleased to express himself and give us in few words the fullest encomium of his adorable body; and it is on the subject of this same sacred and divine flesh that I now mean to entertain you Dear Christians. It is neither of the person of Jesus Christ, nor of his divinity, nor of his soul I am about to speak, but purely of his flesh. And to come at once to the point in hand, I must beg of you to make this remark with me, that the Son of God, in the words of my text, desirous of recommending his body to the Jews does not tell them it is the Temple of the Holy Ghost, or the sanctuary of the Deity, or that it is the master-piece from the hands of the Almighty, but calls it a nourishment and food. "My flesh is meat indeed." However, to consider it under this state of food and nourishment, you'll say, is it not the most imperfect? Oh true, Christians, if we take it in the light of common food, made use of to repair the strength of our bodies and to support nature. But to consider it a sacramental food, a food, all material as it is, that has the virtue to confer on us grace, to afford us a life altogether spiritual and supernatural, that can purify and sanctify us, this is what ought to render it infinitely precious and desirable and what crowns its excellence. The design I have in view, may perhaps startle you, but I'll venture to say, if you will but apply yourselves to comprehend it rightly, it will appear to you very suitable to our present mystery and will perfectly correspond to the idea you have of this day's festival. I will shew you that today by excellence is the feast of the body of Jesus Christ, or as it is commonly called, the feast of Corpus Christi. Such is the title wherewith it was first established and to do justice to this title, you shall see that the body of Jesus Christ could not be held in greater veneration, nor be more honoured that it is by the mystery of the Holy Eucharist, which of all others, is the most august and most dignified of our holy religion. For what makes the body of Jesus Christ appear in its greatest lustre, is its having been imparted to the church in the Holy Sacrament of the altar as will appear in the sequel of this discourse. Be pleased to give attention.

It was but consonant to reason and justice the flesh of Jesus Christ should be honoured and that Jesus Christ should himself concur to render it due honour and veneration for two forcible reasons. In the first place, the honour he did this flesh by contracting so close an alliance with it, by uniting it to his divine person in the Incarnation. And secondly, the extreme humiliations to which he had reduced it in his passion. Did you ever take notice, Dear Christians, of a notable expression in the first chapter of Saint John in expressing the mystery of the Word Incarnate? He does not say the Word was made man, he does not say it was allied to an intelligent and spiritual nature like unto that of angels, or that it took a soul similar to ours, but he simply says "The Word was made flesh." What! cries out Saint Austin, with amaze. The flesh of man and that which in man is the most imperfect, is in what man resembles the brute animal; why then to appropriate to the flesh alone this astonishing mystery of the union made betwixt man and God? Ah! replies his holy doctor, 'tis in order to teach us what God has done for us, what he would become for our sakes, what lengths he would go in being annihilated for us, seeing that God as he was, he did not disdain to make himself flesh. It is true, Dear Christians, but thereby also the Holy Ghost has given us to understand, what was of great importance for us to know. I mean the great dignity of the flesh of Jesus Christ; for in consequence of those divine words, "The Word was made flesh." It may be said agreeable to every principle of divinity and faith, that the flesh of Jesus Christ is the flesh of a God, that is has subsisted by the substance of a God, that it made a part of the whole, which was God; and that as the Word by incarnating itself became flesh, also the flesh of man by the Incarnation became the flesh of a God. From whence we may conclude then that there is no degree of glory or worship which is not strictly due to the flesh of Jesus Christ, and that Jesus Christ himself after so noble an alliance cannot do too much to honour his flesh.

The more so indeed, as in his passion he reduced it to the utmost humiliation, for it is this venerable flesh of his that was overwhelmed for us with ignominies and sufferings. It was that was buffeted and torn with whips, the same that was prophaned by the hands of the common executioners. And to say all in one word, if I may be allowed the expression, it was that which took upon it the whole burthen of our redemption. It was not the soul of Jesus Christ that administered as a victim for our salvation, no, it was his body, it was his virginal, his unspotted flesh. It was that he immolated on the altar of the cross. It was holy and he suffered it to be accursed and a subject of malediction, it was deserving of all kind of respect from men and he permitted it to be exposed to every kind of insult. It was right then he should recompense it and have it honoured in proportion to the outrages it had suffered, or rather in as much as he himself had humbled it. Now this is precisely what Jesus Christ has done in the Holy Eucharist; that was his main view in the instituting this mystery and for this reason it is we celebrate to day the feast of his sacred body.

[In effect, Dear Christians, the Eucharist alone confers more honour on the flesh of Jesus Christ than all the other glorious mysteries of this God made man. Even when he came forth from the sepulchre, the glory he communicated to his body was not to be compared to that he gave it and continues yet daily to give it in his Holy Sacrament. This proposition may appear new, but if you'll pay attention, I'll shew you to a demonstration the truth of it. I admit that Jesus Christ in rising from his tomb communicated to his sacred flesh those admirable qualities of impassibility, subtility, agility and splendour, but these qualities, after all, have nothing that surpasses the bounds of a creature, whereas here—that is to say, in the adorable Eucharist— the flesh of the Saviour is elevated to an order altogether divine. It there takes a being, it there acquires properties, it does there what God can only do, to unfold and explain the whole of which would run me now to too great a length. However, I'll dwell on what is the most essential and what ought to strike you most. It is needless to tell you Christians that this blessed flesh possesses a kind of immensity in the august Sacrament of the altar, for it is certain that it is not bounded there by any space and that in virtue of this mystery it may be at one and the same time in every part of the world, a quality proper to God. I don't tell you only it becomes there quite spiritual, but far otherwise than in its resurrection, because the flesh of Jesus Christ, residing in the host after a spiritual manner, is all in all and all in each part, a miraculous quality peculiar to it. I omit an observation made by the Abbey Rupert, that it is eternal as it is were and incorruptable in the Sacrament, because it will remain there to the end of time, or rather to Christians, that it dies there dayly, but a death a thousand time more wonderful than the immortality even it enjoys in heaven, because it is there to be reborn and received continually by the words of consecration. All which are so many effects of the divine omnipotence to honour the body of our Saviour.]

But the grand miracle, which comprehends all the rest and that which Jesus Christ has marked out to us more expressly in the Gospel, [what men make the least reflection on, but what ought to be the most constant subject of our meditation] and what I find incontestably the most glorious to the flesh of the Son of God, is this, that the flesh of Jesus Christ in the Eucharist, is the food and nourishment of our souls, although it be as to its accidents but a material and earthly substance, it has the virtue and efficacy to enliven our spirits. Instead of the spirit's naturally enlivening the flesh as it ought, here by a most surprising prodigy, the flesh vivify's the spirit, supports it, animates it, and serves it as food for its preservation. For take notice I pray, it is a reflection of Saint Ambrose, when the Son of God spoke to the Jews concerning this Sacrament, he did not say to them "I am meat," but he said "my flesh is meat," the food with which you must be nourished spiritually. It is neither the soul nor the divinity of Jesus Christ, which forms our spiritual nourishment in the Eucharist, it is his flesh, "my flesh" says the text. If the soul and divinity be there present it is, as divines express it, by concomitance. That which nourishes us and which is expressly given in quality of food, is the flesh of this God made man, with which our souls are strengthened and supported, and as Tertullian says, are fattened. Oh! What an honour must here accrue to this divine flesh! That it should be that, which renders us all spiritual, that which communicates grace and which makes us live the life of God himself. Yes Dear Christians, I repeat it, this miracle alone raises the flesh of the Saviour of the world to a supernatural and eminent degree. For none but the flesh of a God could operate such wonders, and God taking it upon himself, could not confer on it greater honour and lustre than by empowering it to produce the like effects. Now all this agrees admirably with the flesh of Jesus Christ in the Eucharist, and is what the church expresses in few words, when it is presented to the faithful by the hands of the priest *Corpus Domini nostri etc.* Receive, Christians, it says to us, receive the body of thy Lord and thy God, and why? To the end he may preserve thy soul unto eternal life. Do you see here, Dear Christians, the inestimable prerogative of the body of Jesus Christ? In the order of nature it is the soul's business to preserve the body, but in the order of grace, it is the body of Jesus Christ preserves our souls. And this order, which is an order of grace in our regard, with respect to Jesus Christ's body, is an order of glory, but of a glory the most eminent and most sublime.

After this, can we be surprised Dear Christians, that God, by a wonderful display of his wisdom and a merciful disposition of his providence should propose this body to be adored in our churches and upon our altars? To whom shall we render more justly this worship of adoration than to a flesh which is the very principle of our life and immortality? And where shall we with more reason adore it than in his Sacrament, since there it is, God has rendered it all powerful and ever at hand to fortify us with the life of grace and animate us according to the Spirit. Yes, my bretheren, says Saint Ambrose, one of the holy Fathers of the third century, we adore still to this day the flesh of our Redeemer and we adore it in the mysteries himself has instituted and which are daily celebrated upon our altars. These words truly home and cutting to our adversaries and which at all times have cast them into strange perplexities. This flesh of Jesus Christ, continues Saint Ambrose, has been formed of earth as well as our ours, and the earth in Holy Writ is called the footstool of the feet of God. But this footstool considered in the person of our Saviour and in the sacrament of his flesh, is more venerable than the thrones of princes, and for that it is we adore it. I knew not, adds Saint Austin, what God "meant to say by his prophet David in the ninety-ninth psalm when he orders us to 'adore his footstool,' and I did not comprehend how it could be done without impiety, but I have discovered the secret of the mystery in the Sacrament of Jesus Christ. For it is what we do daily when we partake of his flesh, as before receiving we adore it, not only without superstition, but with all the merit of faith, because this sacred flesh being a food of salvation—tho' it be of earth and even the stool of God's feet—it should be adored. And so far from sin are we in adoring it, it should be a sin not to adore it." Thus Saint Austin.

For this reason it is, Dear Christians, the church has instituted this feast, which we solemnize under the title to the honour of Christ's body. In the doing of which she has but acted conformably to the sentiments and example of Jesus Christ himself. Christ has been pleased to honour his flesh in the Eucharist and the church honours the Eucharist in order to honour this same flesh.

It might be asked what foundation is there for that ceremony usually practiced on this day in Catholic countries, in carrying our Saviour's body in procession and pomp. I answer many solid and moving reasons vouch for the practice. First, as a very learned divine remarks, in memory of his having carried himself, when he distributed his own flesh and blood to his apostles. For then it is evident, says Saint Austin, he carried his own proper body and that what Scripture said of David in a figurative sense, to wit, that he carried himself in his hands, was fulfilled to the letter in the person of our Saviour. But what did Christ do, when he thus carried himself? He made as I may say a triumph to himself, for he could not be carried more honourably than by himself and in his own hands. Now this is the mystery the church represents to the faithful on this day in causing this venerable body to be carried by the hands of priests, who are as it were the proper hands of the Son of God. But why is it carried out of the church, why in

the streets and publick places? It is, as the same holy
Father observes, by way of thanksgiving for his going
himself formerly, visiting the towns and villages, his making the tour of Judea and Gallilee curing the sick as he
passed, as is mentioned in the ninth chapter of Saint Matthew. 'Tis for this the church has him carried thro' all
Christendom, hoping at the same time he will be graciously
pleased to work amongst us the same wonders he wraught
in favour of the Jews. Blessed Francis Sales gives this also
a reason: The church ordains the carrying this sacred
pledge to make him an authentic reparation for all the
insults and indignities he suffered in the streets of Jerusalem where he was dragged from place to place, from
tribunal to tribunal. In satisfaction for such injuries he is
carried publickly, followed by the people with acclamations
and canticles of joy.

But another reason above all I must not omit, and which
may serve for your instruction, Dear Christians. By these
processions the church intends the reparation of the many
outrages and irreverences bad Christians have made him
and continue to cause him in the Sacrament of the Eucharist. Yes, it is for our selves the church has established this
festival of way of making him becoming amends. It is for
all our prophanations, for all our sacriledges, it is for all
our irreverences at church and before the altar of Jesus
Christ and in his sanctuary. It is for all the scandals we
have given him, for all the unworthy Communions of so
many hypocritical sinners, for all the Masses celebrated by
bad priests, for all our tepidity and coolness in appoaching
the holy table and for all the negligencies just souls even
may bring with them. Yes Christians, it is for yours and
mine, for the many ingratitudes we have for so many years
been guilty of in frequenting this Mystery of love. It is on
our account these processions were ordained to the end the
honour thereby rendered to the sacred flesh of our Redeemer, may in some measure compensate for the indigni-

ties received from us to this time, and which every day it continues to receive, and what is horrid to think, even far worse than what it received from the Jews in his passion. For in his passion it suffered but for a time, but here it is exposed to suffer while the world lasts. In his passion it suffered but as much as Jesus was willing it should and because he was willing, but here it suffers, I may say, by force and violence. If it suffered in his passion, it was in a state of nature passible and mortal, but here his sacred flesh suffers in a state even of impassibility. What it suffered in his passion was glorious to God and salutary to man, but what it suffers in the Eucharist is both pernicious to men, and injurious to God. These powerful motives Dear Christians, ought to awaken and rouse all the energy and devotion towards this great mystery.

The occupation then of a Christian soul during this octave should be to enter as much as possible into the views and sentiments of the church and joyn with it in honouring this adorable flesh of the Redeemer. That is to say, in rendering it all the homage in our power in the Sacrament of the altar, imitating Mary Magdalen whose zeal towards it was remarkable, watering it with her tears, wiping it with her hair, and anointing it with perfumes. An exercise, says Saint Thomas, the Son of God commended, how averse so ever he might have been to the delicacies of life. And why? Because he delighted in seeing his flesh honoured. Let us, Dear Christians, with the same spirit prostrate ourselves in this sacred presence and there offer him a thousand sacrifices of praise, of interior adoration and thanksgiving, addressing him with a lively and ardent faith. My adorable Saviour Jesus Christ, true God and true man, I believe firmly your sacred flesh is here present under the vail and species of the Sacrament. I adore you with all the extent of my soul as my Sovereign Lord, with all the respect I possibly can and with joy to depend on you as your creature and slave redeemed with the infinite price of your death.

As you have the goodness to remain with us, Dear Lord, I should be most ungrateful and a bitter enemy to my own happiness was I to refuse the honour you do me in suffering me to come before you. I confess my God, I have stray'd from you by my iniquities and richly deserve to be denied a hearing. Neither should I have the temerity to appear in your sacred presence, had I not heard your amiable voice calling on all miserable forlorn souls, saying to them: "Come unto me all you that labour and are burthened, and I'll refresh you." I come then, Lord, at you word, I confide in the fidelity of your promises. I come to cast myself at your feet as in an inviolable place of refuge, where I hope to meet with the assurance of my salvation and the abolition of my crimes. I come to make you a protestation anew, but in good earnest and forever, of my fidelity in your service and to renew the alliance I have had the honour to contract with you in my baptism, and which I have so often broken by my rebellious conduct. Hitherto I have been insensible of your interests, but I now begin to be moved at the injuries done you in your adorable Sacrament, at so many profanations in war, so many sacrileges, irreverences and indignities committed by the enemies of the Church, by Catholics, in your temples, at holy Mass, in Communions, at the foot of your altar in the persons of your priests. Such are the sentiments, Dear Christians, may God in his mercy inspire you with. May his holy name be for ever blessed, and this Divine Sacrament of his sacred flesh be honoured more and more throughout every nation of the earth. It is my sincere wish. *In nomine Patris, et Filii, et Spiritu Sancti, Amen.*

HENRY PILE
Corpus Christi

*Henry Pile was born in Maryland on May 24, 1743
and entered the Society of Jesus on September 7, 1761.
After the suppression of the Jesuits in 1773, Pile remained in England ministering for many years in the
Yorkshire District. He did not return to Maryland until
July 1784. He appears to have spent most of his
ministry at Newport in Charles County. He died in
1814. This undated sermon fragment was meant to be
used on the Feast of Corpus Christi.*

In Festo Corpus Christi

> *Accipite et comedite, hoc est corpus meum.*
> "Take and eat, this is my body."

The mystery the holy Catholick Church celebrates today,
is a memorial and abridgement of the wonderful works of
God. It is the masterpiece of his love and wisdom. Not
content with having become man and died upon a cross for
our redemption; he would also remain with us to the end of
the world to be the food and nourishment of our souls. In
what manner does he remain with us? Besides his ordinary
providence, which every moment watches over us and
keeps us from falling into our nothingness, besides the
graces and inspirations he daily sends us, besides the
invisible assistance of the Holy Ghost, which will abide
with his Church through all ages; he still remains with us in
a more familiar manner on our altars, where he invites us
not only to converse with him as a friend, but to receive
him into our breasts. For in the blessed Eucharist is contained really the true body and blood, soul and divinity of
our Saviour Jesus Christ under the appearance of bread and
the same under the appearance of wine, for the spiritual

nourishment of our souls, so that the priest, though he receives under both kinds, receives no more than the layman, who only receives under one kind. This divine sacrament has many different names, which both express the grandeur and excellance of it and shew the noble and heavenly effect if causes. It is called Eucharist, which word signifies grace or thanksgiving; because it confers grace to our souls and is offered to God in thanksgiving in the sacrifice of Mass. It is called sacrament of the altar, because it is there offered and consecrated and kept for the use of the faithful. It is stiled Holy Sacrament, because it is more holy and august than the other sacraments; because it not only confers grace to those that worthily receive it, but also contains really the author of all grace and sanctity, Jesus Christ. We call it the bread of infants, because to eat of it worthily, we must be children of God, that is, in the state of grace. We stile it the bread of angels, because to draw nourishment to our souls from it, we must approach it with the purity of angels.

INDEX OF SCRIPTURAL CITATIONS

Leviticus 10, 159
Leviticus 12:6, 91
Deuteronomy 25:2, 145
II Kings 1:9, (II Samuel), 146
III Kings 2, (I Kings), 185
IV Kings 13, (II Kings), 198
Judith 8:22, 143
Judith 8:27, 146
Job 13:15, 143
Job 21:13, 145
Psalms 21:7, 142
Psalms 26:3, 144
Psalms 44, 188
Psalms 44:11, 180
Psalms 67, 196, 198
Psalms 99, 207
Psalms 103, 154
Psalms 107:1, 147
Psalms 118:137, 146
Psalms 138, 194
Wisdom 3:5, 143
Wisdom 3:6, 143
Matthew 3:33, 149
Matthew 5:10, 147
Matthew 5:11, 142
Matthew 5:12, 148
Matthew 7:14, 148
Matthew 7:15, 66
Matthew 9, 208
Matthew 10:22, 148
Matthew 10:28, 144
Matthew 11, 156

Matthew 11:12, 148
Matthew 13:31, 62, 139
Matthew 13:44, 62
Matthew 16:13, 62, 64
Matthew 16:24, 149
Matthew 18, 64, 163
Matthew 18:17, 63
Matthew 24:13, 148
Matthew 26, 31, 152
Matthew 26:42, 146
Matthew 28:20, 64
Luke 5:21, 79
Luke 6:23, 148
Luke 14:16, 151
Luke 14:16–24, 29
Luke 16, 64
Luke 16:25, 145, 146
Luke 21:17, 142
John 6, 154–155
John 6:54, 156
John 6:55, 201
John 6:56–59, 29, 44
John 8:7, 145
John 10:16, 63
John 11:16, 144
John 13, 161, 163
John 14:16–17, 64
John 15, 195
John 15:13, 143
John 18:36, 61
Acts 2:5, 72
Acts 5, 198
Romans 8:38, 150

I Corinthians 5:1–2, 71
I Corinthians 6, 198
I Corinthians 11:23–29, 29, 39
I Corinthians 11:28, 159
Galatians 2, 196
Galatians 2:20, 162
Ephesians 4, 65
Philippians 4:13, 150

I Thessalonians 1:6, 140
I Thessalonians 2:6, 73
II Timothy 2:5, 148
II Timothy 3:12, 149
II Timothy 4:7, 147
Revelation 2, 162
Revelation 3:19, 141
Revelation 21:2, 63

GENERAL INDEX

Altham, John, 56
Ambrose, St., 161, 199, 205, 206
Antonelli, Leonardo, 18
Aquinas, St. Thomas, 9, 29
Askmore, MD, 179
Assumption Cathedral, Baltimore, MD, 87, 102
Attwood, Peter, 88, 93, 98, 99
Augustine, St., 35, 36, 41, 142, 156, 198, 202

Basil, St., 180
Bellarmine, St. Robert, 9
Berington, Joseph, 4, 14, 18
Bernard, St., 148, 180, 181, 184
Bitouzey, Germain Barnabas, 57, 66, 68
Boarman, John, 57, 70, 88
Boarman, Sylvester, 57
Bohemia, MD, 57, 78, 179
Bohemia Academy, 107
Bolton, John, 31, 35, 36, 48, 49, 88, 92, 93, 95, 96, 97, 100, 137, 179–210
Boone, John, 57, 62, 80, 169–178
Boone's Chapel, MD, 169
Bossuet, Jacques Benigne, 60
Brooke Family, 58
Bruges (Jesuit college), 108
Burke, Edmund, 8

Calvert, Cecil, 56
Calvin, John, 76
Carey, Patrick, 3

Carmelites, 83
Carroll Family, 58
Carroll, Charles, of Carrollton, 83, 108, 179
Carroll, Daniel, 83, 108
Carroll, James, 57
Carroll, John, 57, 58, 59, 61, 66, 67, 69, 71, 107–110; and American Church government 11–12; anti-Roman feeling 15; and Catholic emancipation 10–11; and celibacy 14; and Deism 112–115; and devotion to the Sacred Heart 13; and education 4; and enlightened despotism 9; and Febronianism 9, 10, 11; as Federalist 7; and French Revolution 8; and Gallicanism 11; on impersonality of God 116–118; and Jansenism 13; relations with other Jesuits 6, 17; and restoration of Jesuits 19–20; on liberty 7; on liturgy 16; and Marian devotion 94, 98, 100–101, 102; on perfectability of man 118–125; preaching of 82, 88; relations with Propaganda Fide 12, 13, 16, 17; and religious intolerance 14–15; and Thomism 6–7, 14; and trusteeism 8–9; on U.S. Constitution 10; on universal religion 125–130
Cause, John, 61

215

Charles III, emperor, 6
Chinnici, Joseph, 1, 3
Civil Constitution of the Clergy, 8
Clement V, pope, 28
Clement XIV, pope, 15, 70, 108
Condorcet, Jean, 121, 122, 126
Conewago, PA, 151
Confirmation, sacrament of, 66
Cornwallis' Neck, MD, 151, 167, 179
Corpus Christi (see also Eucharist), 28, 76, 151–166, 201, 202, 211–212; liturgical texts 29; procession 29, 36–37, 48
Council of Trent, 197
Creed; ninth article of 63; tenth article of 78
Curran, Robert Emmett, 3, 73
Cyprian, St., 176–177

Deer Creek, MD, 57
Deism, 112
Diderich, Bernard (John Baptist), 31, 32, 33, 35, 43, 44, 45, 46, 47, 57, 70, 72, 76, 88, 92
Diderot, Denis, 1
Digges Family, 58
Dolan, Jay P., 2
DuBourg, Louis William, 14, 41
Dulles, Avery, 55

Egido, Téofanes, 2
Elder, Mrs., 151, 167
Elizabeth of Hungary, St., 196
Elk River, MD, 57, 76
English Martyrs, 73, 143–144
Eucharist (see also Corpus Christi); Bread of Angels 37, 40; and the Church 201–210; divine immanence in 47; Easter Duty 49; and frequent reception 39–43, 49; as guarantee of eternal life 44–46; *O sacrum convivium* 44, 166; and Penance 39, 49; profanation of 47, 77; and the Psalms 35; Real Presence in 30–

37, 48, 76; reverence for 49; as a source of strength 43–44, 50; *Utraquism* 30; worthiness in reception of 37–39, 49

Farmer, Ferdinand, 57, 58
Febronius, Justinus, 9
Frambach, Augustin James, 31, 34, 37, 38, 39, 40, 41, 43, 44, 45, 49, 151–166
Franklin, Benjamin, 16, 71, 109, 120
Frederick, MD, 151, 167

Gay, Peter, 116, 127
Georgetown University, 17, 83
Gervase, Thomas, 56
Gibbon, Edward, 126
Goetz, John, 5
Goshenhoppen, PA, 36
Gregoire, Henri, 13
Gregory the Great, St., 143

Hanley, Thomas O'Brien, 5
Heilbron, John Charles, 6
Hennesey, James, 2
Henry VIII, king, 10, 78
Holy Name, feast of, 63
Holy Trinity, Philadelphia, PA, 18, 61
Hontheim, Johann Nikolaus von, 9
Hume, David, 113, 116, 126
Hunter, George, 57, 73

Jansenism, 39
Jefferson, Thomas, 71, 109, 116, 125
Jenkins, Augustine, 57, 70, 78, 89
Jerome, St., 195
Jesuits; and converts 73; education of 59; preaching 60; relations with Protestants 73–80; American vocations 59
Joseph II, emperor, 5, 9, 10
Jubilee Year, 70

Kant, Immanuel, 112, 120
Kentucky, 83
Kulturkampf, 65

Lent, 74
Lessing, Gotthold, 125
Lewis, John, 88, 90, 91, 92, 96, 97
Liège (Jesuit college), 7, 14, 108
Locke, John, 110, 111
Luther, Martin, 32, 76, 77, 79

Manners, Matthias, 57, 78
Marks of the Church, 75, 76
Martin of Tours, St., 196
Mary, Blessed Virgin; Assumption of 92, 95, 98, 179, 180–193; in economy of salvation 90–94; *Hail Mary* 101; and Incarnation 89, 90; in life of the Church 95–101; *Magnificat* 98; and the Passion of Christ 89–90; as patroness of Baltimore diocese 101; Purification of 90, 96; and the Rosary 94, 97, 102, 179, 188–193; and the saints 194–200; sodality of 96, 191
Maryland Mission, 56–60
Maryland Penal Laws, 107
McConchies, MD, 139
McKenzie, John L., 61
Medley's Neck, MD, 179, 201
Milner, John, 10
Molyneux, Robert, 57, 71
Mosley, Joseph, 57, 58, 69, 73, 75, 137, 139–150

Napoleon, emperor, 19
Neale, Henry, 57, 61, 79, 80
Neale, Leonard, 57, 62
Newport, MD, 179, 180, 211
Newton, Isaac, 111, 116
Newtown, MD, 57, 62, 78, 80, 82, 169, 179

O'Brien, David, 3
Olaechea, Rafael, 2

Paine, Thomas, 71, 109, 111
Patuxents, 56
Pellentz, James, 151
Penance, sacrament of, 78
Peter Damian, St., 93, 181, 186
Philosophical Society of Philadelphia, 58
Pile, Henry, 30, 57, 63, 74, 76, 211–212
Piscataways, 56
Pius VII, pope, 18, 19
Plongeron, Bernard, 1
Plowden, Charles, 4, 5, 7
Pomfret, MD, 151, 166
Port Tobacco, MD, 57, 82, 179, 180
Potomac, MD, 57
Prince Georges County, MD, 169
Protestant beliefs, 68–69

Raynal, Guillaume, 5
Reign of Terror, 65
Reuter, Caesarius, 13
Ricci, Scipione de, 1, 15
Roche, Daniel, 2
Rock Creek, MD, 108
Roels, Benjamin Louis, 31, 40, 41, 43, 44, 57, 64, 65, 82
Rosaryville, MD, 169
Rousseau, Jean Jacques, 120

Sacred Heart, devotion to, 70
St. Francis Xavier, feast of, 169, 170
St. Inigoes, MD, 57, 82, 151, 169
St. Joseph, Cordova, MD (see also Tuckahoe), 139, 179, 180, 201
St. Joseph, Philadelphia, PA, 57
St. Mary's Seminary, Baltimore, MD, 37
St. Omers (Jesuit college), 7, 107, 108, 139
Sakia, MD, 57, 69, 179, 180
Sales, St. Francis de, 36, 60, 208
Seton, St. Elizabeth, 41

Sewall, Charles, 30, 38, 39, 40, 41, 44, 46, 57, 71, 77
Sign of the Cross, 69
Socinius, Faustus, 13
Socrates, 113
Suárez, Francisco, 9
Synod of Baltimore, 101
Synod of Pistoia, 13

Taney, Roger Brooke, 58, 83
Tindal, Matthew, 116, 118, 119
Toland, John, 125
Tuckahoe, MD (see also St. Joseph, Cordova), 57, 82

University of Pennsylvania, 58

Voltaire, Francois-Marie, 1, 111, 125

Watten (Jesuit novitiate), 7, 108, 179
Weishaupt, Adam, 5
Wharton, Charles, 6
White, Andrew, 56
White Marsh, MD, 57
Williams, John, 57, 63
Wye, MD, 57